The Garden

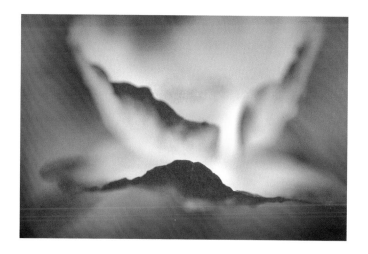

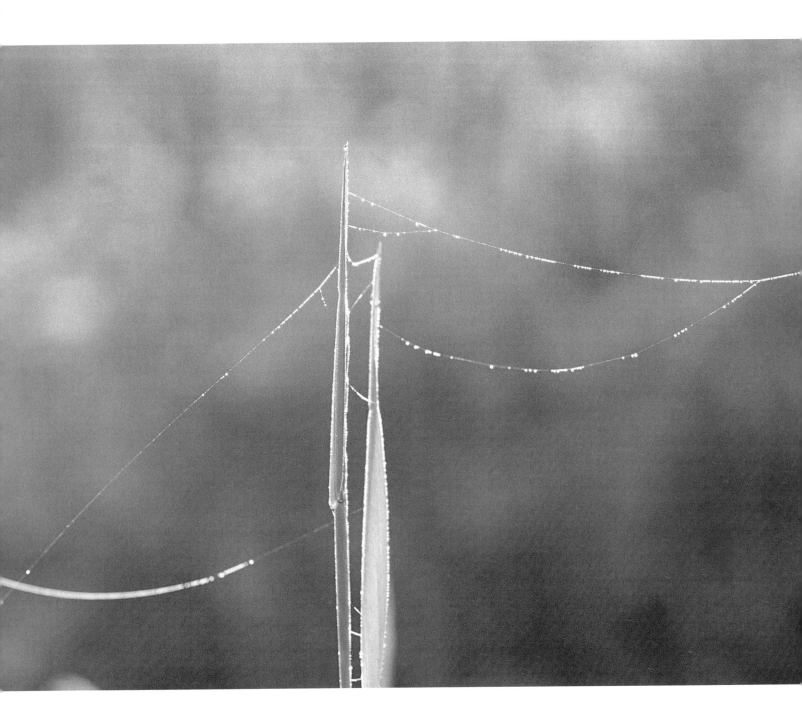

The Garden

Freeman Patterson

KEY PORTER BOOKS

National Library of Canada Cataloguing in Publication

Patterson, Freeman
        The garden / Freeman Patterson

ISBN 1-55263-517-1

        1. Gardens--Pictorial works. I. Title.

TR662.P38 2003   779'.97126   C2002-906060-53

The publisher gratefully acknowledges the support of the Canada Council for the Arts and the Ontario Arts Council for its publishing program. We acknowledge the support of the Government of Ontario through the Ontario Media Development Corporation's Ontario Book Initiative.

We acknowledge the financial support of the Government of Canada through the Book Publishing Industry Development Program (BPIDP) for our publishing activities.

Key Porter Books Limited
70 The Esplanade
Toronto, Ontario
Canada M5E 1R2
www.keyporter.com

Editor: Clare McKeon
Editorial Assistant: Janie Yoon
Design: Peter Maher
Color separations: Quadratone Graphics Ltd./Tom Childs
Scans: Dave Carson

03 04 05 06 07 08 6 5 4 3 2 1
Printed and bound in Canada

For

JOANNE,

my good friend and fellow gardener,

and in fond memory of

LYNDA,

another friend who gardened with me.

ACKNOWLEDGMENTS

My deepest thanks to Nina for your ideas and constructive suggestions
about this book and for your warm support always.

Gratitude beyond measure to Dr. Jim Collings, my family doctor;
Dr. Florence Wong of the Toronto Hospital; Dr. Kevork Peltekian,
Dr. Vivian McAlister, and the amazing staff of the Atlantic Health Sciences
Centre, especially its Liver Transplant Clinic; and Olga Cruz who, working in
so many different ways, saved my life and restored me to good health.
Without your efforts this book could never have been created.

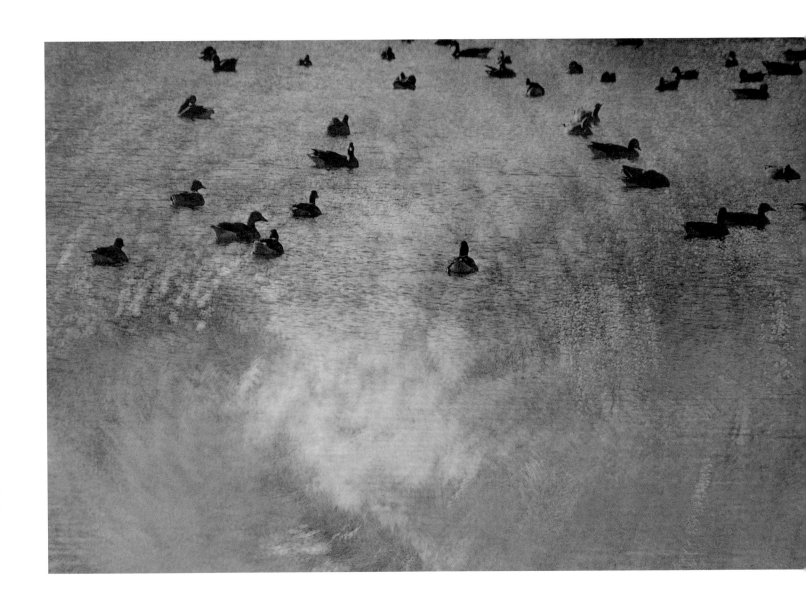

PREFACE

Every garden and every gardener is a work in progress. And no matter how tiny or grand, how colorful or restrained, how wild or ordered, the garden is a metaphor for the gardener. When you invite somebody into your garden you are inviting them to meet you.

Although our garden may be like a "persona," one facet of our personality that we want the world to see, more likely it is the face that we, as gardeners, want to show ourselves. So, when we observe and contemplate our creation carefully, we can learn a great deal both about who we are and who we want to be.

I am forever gardening in my imagination. Have you ever met a gardener who isn't? I don't mean creating scenarios that we would like to reproduce in the physical world, but gardens we can never create and probably nobody else could, either — even if our financial resources were unlimited and our patience endless. But, perhaps we will draw or paint our imaginary gardens or, in my case, create them as photographs.

For example, I'm sure that somewhere there is a small lake like this one — a pond where, even now, a flock of geese is swimming among the reflections of spring flowers on the water's surface. I can't find it at Shamper's Bluff; none of the ponds are quite like this, and none of the reflections will ever look quite like these. And yet, it exists — first in my

imagination, second in a photograph, and now in this book
— and we all can pause by its banks and find awe and delight
in its beauty.

Because every garden is a place of dreams and every
gardener a dreamer, we should find nothing strange and much
that is symbolic in our own and other gardens. Are the paths
straight, or do they curve and wander? What colors appear
consistently? Does the gardener worry about ripping out every
last weed?

When we want to learn something important about
ourselves, it's a good idea to go into our garden. We'll find
that we've planted a lot of answers there.

INTRODUCTION

Shamper's Bluff is a high, forested, rocky peninsula that juts into Belleisle Bay in New Brunswick's lower St. John River valley. Perhaps five hundred acres (two hundred hectares) in size, about half of the bluff is now a private ecological reserve belonging to the Nature Conservancy of Canada. This reserve is my home, as I donated most of the land to the Conservancy in return for life tenancy. Its several ecological zones or natural habitats are home for 253 species of plants, flocks of migratory and nonmigratory birds, and mammals such as hares, foxes, field mice, coyotes, flying squirrels, deer, and occasionally moose and bear. Of course, there are also toads, frogs, salamanders, garter snakes, fish swimming in the water lapping the bluff, and insect species far too numerous to count. All of these species have an aboriginal claim to the ecological diversity of Shamper's Bluff. They were here long before me or any of the other forty or so human residents.

In a circle of about twenty-five acres (ten hectares) around my house, I have the privilege of engaging with the land and the many plant and animal species in a restricted but active way. I can, for example, mow paths through the fields for easy access to the succession of wildflowers. I may cut alder bushes growing in the nearby swamp so the numerous clumps of cinnamon and interrupted ferns can continue to build vigorously the gigantic tussocks they commenced over a century ago. I am permitted to blaze a trail for wandering to the edge of the swamp, where I have placed a bench for sitting and observing the waving sea of green. All those really important things!

Near my house, barn, and guest cottage, I am able to mix the wild and the domesticated with abandon. Here, in an area with no defined boundaries, a mélange of flower beds overflows with both annual and perennial plants, and paths with no apparent destination meander through spirea, wild rhododendron, and blueberry bushes. Here native ox-eye daisies dance with the red poppies of Tuscany, Israel, and Flanders, broad-leaved hostas clump together in the shade of wild apple and birch trees, and perky blue forget-me-nots poke through sweeping expanses of hay-scented ferns.

But this is not a garden of Eden where life is care free and lived unconsciously. It lives and grows in the "real" world — in the objective world of my senses, in colors and tones, scents and fragrances, bird songs and buzzes of insects, and in the subjective world of my feelings, nourished by the sunlight and rain of my emotions, fertilized by my imagination, reveries, and dreams. The sense of fullness and satisfaction I experience from both aspects of this world requires cultivation, fertilization, pruning, and other hard work.

For many years I planned and tended my garden alone, but as it grew larger and I grew weaker due to a long, debilitating illness, I began to teach an interested long-time friend, Joanne, about plants and their lives, about gardening with native plants as well as "domesticated" species, about the importance of being sensitive to microclimates and weather, to soil types and conditions, and about observing natural designs of every sort.

When I became very ill, Joanne assumed all the gardening responsibilities, though I could never resist making suggestions. And, as her knowledge and confidence grew, neither could she. Now that I'm healthy and active again, we go about "doing our thing," both together and separately, but our pleasure in the garden and in gardening is greater now because it is always shared.

Gardening together has also deepened our friendship. When Joanne arrives, usually as the early light is just beginning to illuminate the paths that wind through the fields and woods, one of us makes a pot of good coffee and we sit at my kitchen table talking about gardening for ten minutes or, perhaps, an hour. Gardening with plants, gardening with ideas, gardening with dreams. Neither of us is quite sure where the physical garden ends and the spiritual one begins, and neither of us cares. The transition from one to the other is easy and utterly natural.

I invite you to join us in the garden through pictures and words, the entire garden — a communion of habitats, species, and individuals, a place where rain is as important as sunshine, where colors blend seamlessly with fragrances, imagination, and dreams, where everything that lives and grows also dies, but where the cycle of life is eternal.

SPRING

That God once loved a garden

We learn in Holy writ,

And seeing gardens in the Spring

I well can credit it.

WINIFRED MARY LETTS, "Stephen's Green"

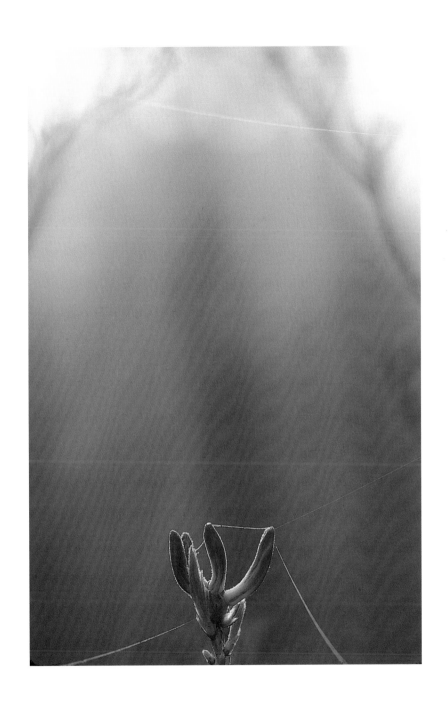

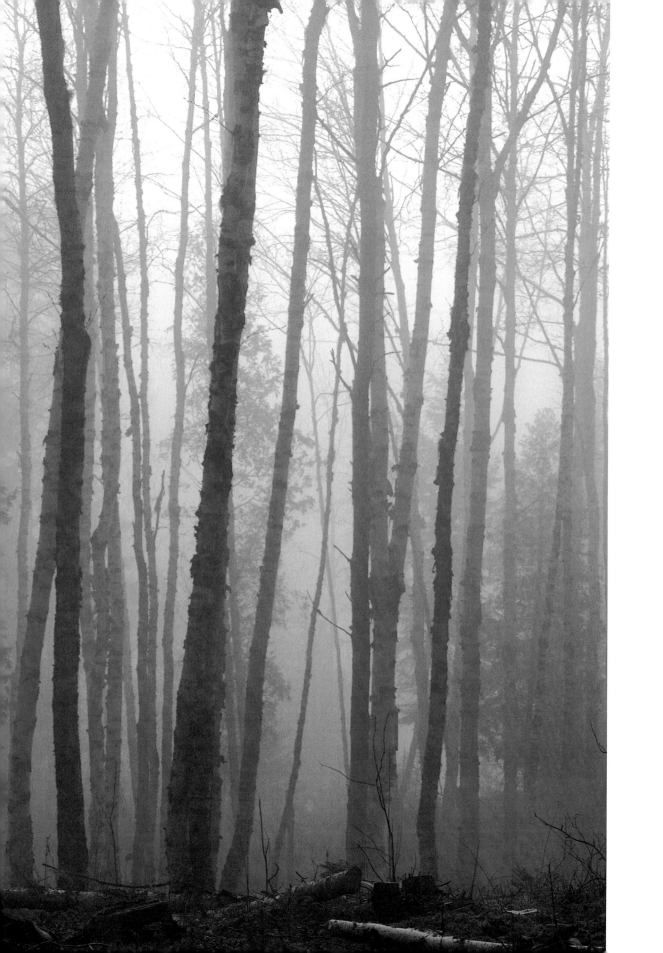

Near dawn on early spring mornings, the difference in temperature between the cold, frozen earth and the warmer air that has caused the snow to melt often produces ground mists. These mists, which obscure the more distant trees in the woods behind my house, usually soften the entire landscape for hours.

When the sun rises unseen above the distant horizon, it briefly transforms the somber, delicate grays into vibrant golds. As it ascends, it gradually dilutes these intensely warm hues to the palest creams. Finally, it emerges as a ghostly orb on a milk-white sea. Then the mist twirls itself into strands and wisps, and dissolves forever.

Out of the mist come flowers. The first tiny greens peek through half-rotted maple and aspen leaves, cedar twigs, and spruce needles, beginning the re-carpeting of the forest floor. Near the guest cottage a purple crocus, nestled against the south-facing side of a large granite boulder, seems to gaze up impudently from its very cozy nook. And the sunny yellow blossoms of coltsfoot light up roadside ditches, making the ten-minute walk to my mailbox a succession of highlights.

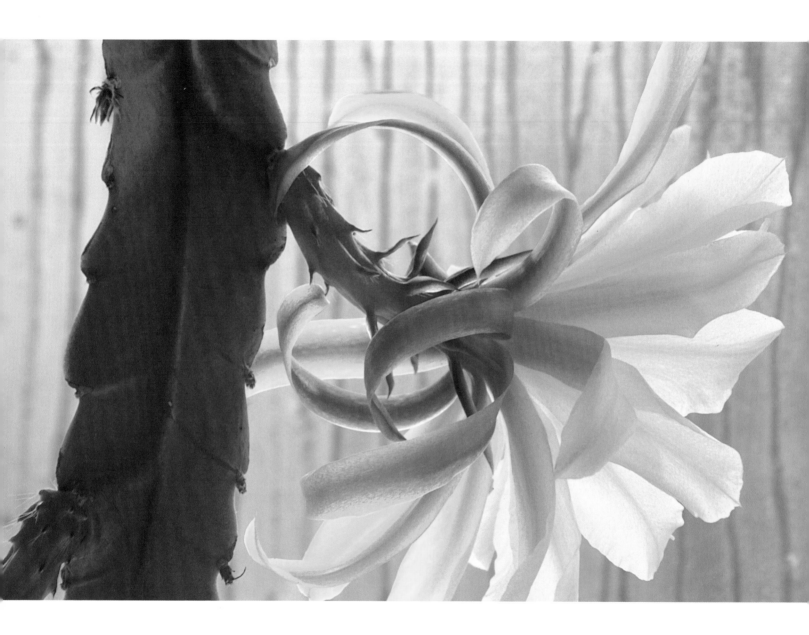

By late winter and very early spring I not only enjoy the flowers blooming in my sunroom, I need them. My sense of well-being depends on having plants living, growing, and blooming around me, especially when there are still none flowering out of doors.

We grow plants, especially flowering plants, in our gardens, greenhouses, and windows because they are beautiful. Beauty never requires justification, because it balances the ugliness, hurt, and sorrow that are present in every human life to a greater or lesser degree. Without beauty as inspiration and refuge, our deprived souls grow hard and cold, and often we transfer, or project, our unacknowledged suffering onto others, especially those with whom we live and work.

Beauty is invariably a positive factor, an enriching presence, a healing influence. It is true in music, painting, and dance, of clouds in the sky and birds singing in the light of dawn, of flowers, even humble geraniums in kitchen windows.

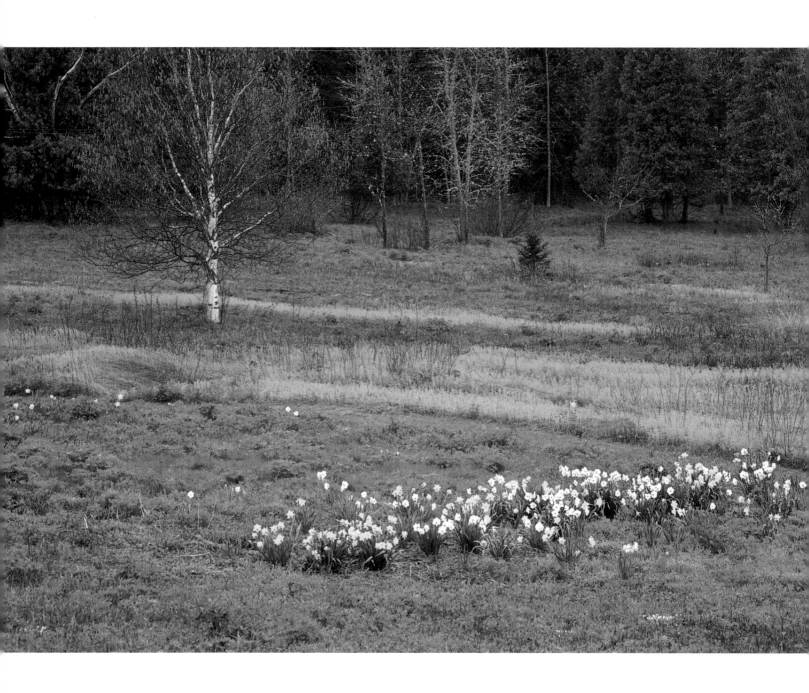

When the leaves on trees are about the size of squirrels' ears, when birds returning from months in the south dart around in search of nesting sites and daffodils dance in gardens and meadows, a deep sense of well-being floods over me. Everything good in the world seems possible.

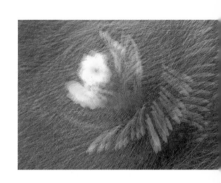

My emotional liberation is mirrored by my increased physical activity. Lying in bed after sunrise is incomprehensible. Politely, but firmly, I refuse to attend meetings, particularly in the evening. I neglect my basement work area, disown my computer, and spend every possible moment outdoors. In short, I make room for receiving the gift of spring.

As I wander along field and forest paths long covered with snow, sniffing the breeze to savor the rich, moist tang of the soil and the drifting ambrosial hints from flowers blooming somewhere, I observe variations of color that appear at no other time of year — delicate, warm, and sprightly hues. I reconnect with Earth and sense the incredible surge of creativity around me, and within me.

And I garden. I can't help it. My whole being longs to be engaged in the birthing process. This is not a hobby, but an essential aspect of who I am. For me, not to garden would be saying "No" to life itself.

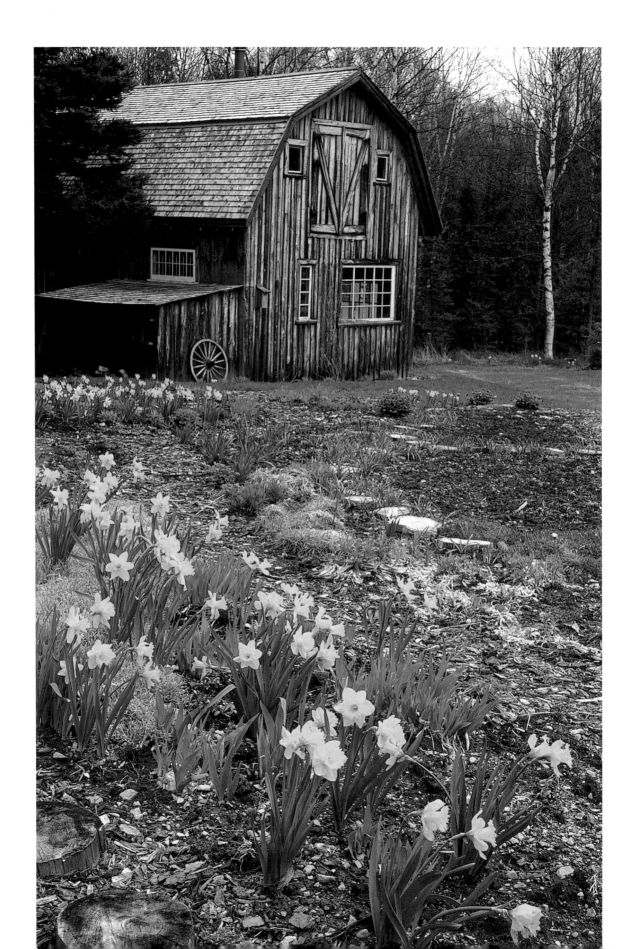

Nearly everybody likes my barn. It can look drab on a damp, cloudy morning, however, and in this picture its drabness is magnified by the way I've juxtaposed the barn with the fresh greens and vibrant yellows.

There's a reason for every composition, but most of the time the reason isn't a conscious one. Rather, the various picture elements look good together in a certain arrangement, or they simply "feel right." Later, when I analyze an image, I can always explain why a shape works well with certain lines, or how I might have improved the overall design. The same is true for my garden. However, my analysis does not explain why I chose to make this particular composition rather than another one. The real reason for every design lies elsewhere.

It lies deep within the creator — somewhere in the unconscious. When it comes to creating a garden, or making pictures of gardens, or making any sort of photograph for that matter, we seldom do the introspection necessary to discover where we are operating from. In analyzing this photograph, I eventually realized that as much as I like my barn, I like the daffodils better. They actually "show up" the barn in this composition. This was my way of acknowledging that my creations are rarely a match for those of nature.

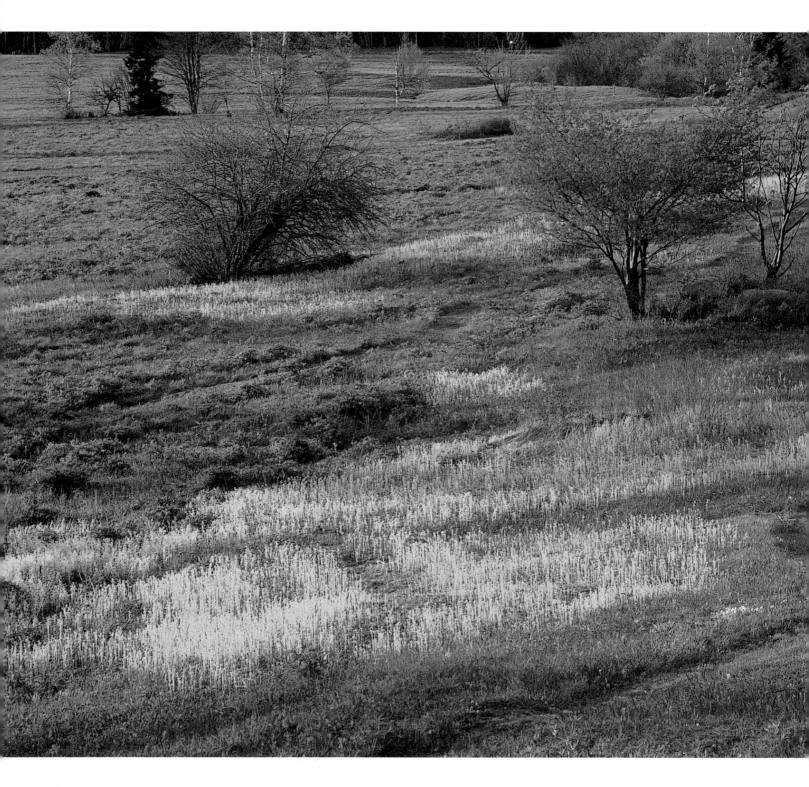

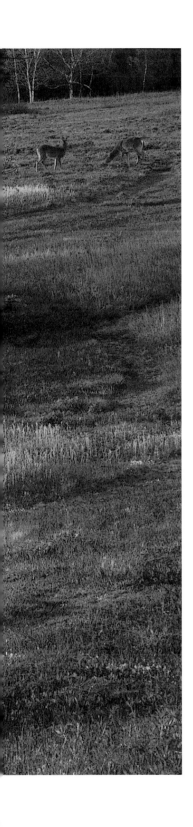

"Spring comes, and the grass grows by itself."
That's a bit of Zen wisdom I quote to myself when I realize
that I'm rushing around trying to do everything at once.

Often we "attack" our gardens in a sort of frenzy. It's all
too easy in spring to become overly enthusiastic, to prepare a
mental or written list of all the jobs that "need" doing, and to
destroy the magnificence of the season by trying to do them
all. What we're really doing, of course, is passing up our
enjoyment of the present in anticipation of a future that, for
one reason or another, may never come. When summer does
arrive, we may well fill it up with another roster of important
tasks, all of which need to be completed before fall comes and
winter sets in. This reminds me of a big sign I once saw in
front of a country pub: "Free beer tomorrow."

The only time to enjoy a beer, or a garden, is now. So,
especially when I've had a busy, full day working in my
gardens, the fields, or the woods, I deliberately give myself a
couple of hours before sunset to sit on my deck and look
down at this scene. Spring changes it daily, even from moment
to moment, as different birds begin to call, or deer emerge
from the forest to graze in the late evening light. It all happens
by itself, but only I can give myself the time to enjoy it.

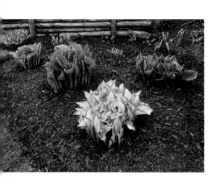

Few activities give me more pleasure than observing the design of natural things and situations. Take this favorite mountain ash tree, for example. When I view it from my front deck, it always appears as a triangle — with its apex at the bottom among the rocks. The most prominent of these rocks is also triangular, pointing upward to the tree. If I want a more symmetrical composition, I'll move my camera position a little to the left, then swing the lens slightly back to the right. This will shift the position of the triangular rock to a spot precisely under the triangular tree. But when I do that, I lose one of the little patches of green leaves that appear in each lower corner of the composition, the one balancing the other. So I have to choose.

The decision I make will probably be based on feeling — which design "feels better"? Thus, in settling on the final composition, I'm also concerned, often quite unconsciously, with the inner me, and the resulting photograph is a description of my meeting with the subject matter. The camera always looks both ways.

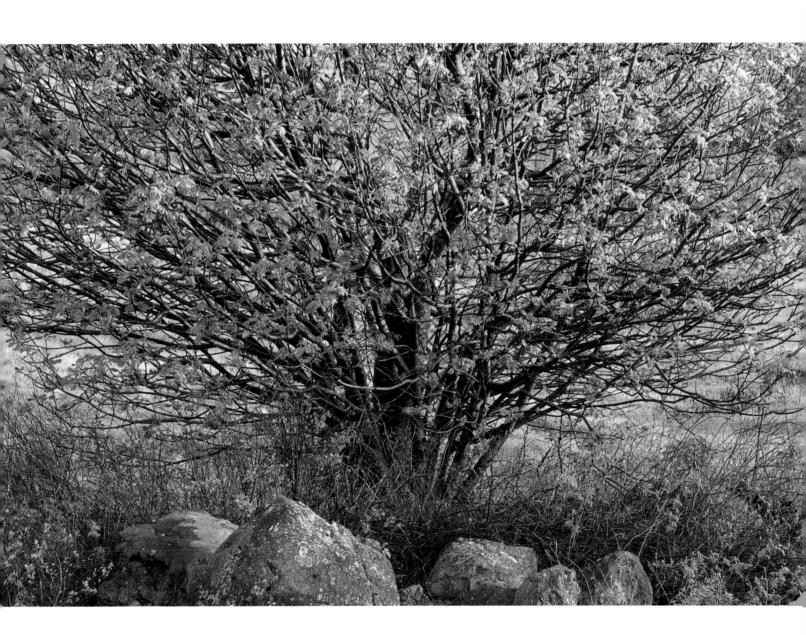

The ways that one generation of a species facilitates the survival of the next is fascinating, and whole careers have been built on such fields of study. Almost without knowing it, gardeners, too, observe and assimilate a considerable amount of information about propagation and survival.

Hay-scented ferns provide a simple example. Every year the young fronds push their way up to the light through a thick blanket of the previous year's dead brown fronds and remnant stalks. The old growth has acted as mulch for the rhizomes, or roots, of the plants, protecting them from even the most frigid winter temperatures. When the new shoots are beginning to stand tall, the warm air and moisture that contribute to their rapid growth also help the old, brown fronds to decay. Before long they rot and become part of the humus, which mixes with and gradually gets absorbed by the soil beneath, enriching it for subsequent generations. The same process is repeated by many, many other species of plants.

Hay-scented ferns, which smell like newly mowed hay when they are crushed, are abundant at Shamper's Bluff. A striking yellow green in early spring, they deepen to mid-green as summer approaches, then turn pale yellow, rich yellow orange, or brown as the autumn passes, always following the sun as it journeys across the sky. Late in October or November, they weaken and collapse, forming the protective cover that will ensure the arrival of their successors.

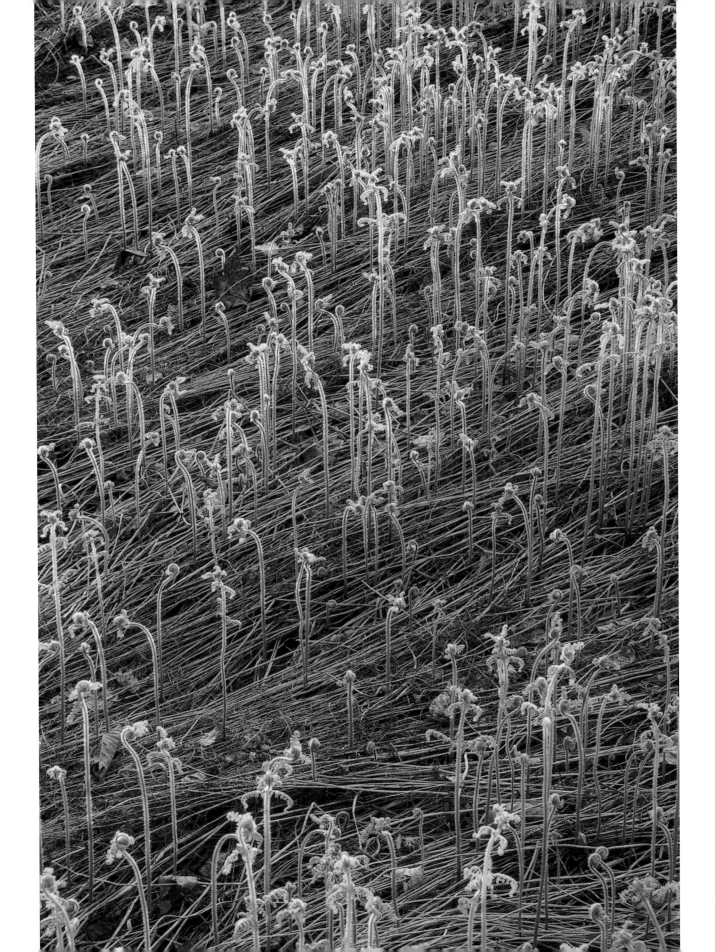

When we listen to its voice, nature often guides our emotions and our behavior. Sometimes it encourages us to jump and shout for joy, and other times it tells us to be still. There is scarcely an emotion that, at one time or another, natural things and situations have not evoked in me. This no longer surprises me at all. The renowned eco-theologian, Father Thomas Berry, encourages us to think of nature not as a collection of objects, but rather as a communion of subjects. We are all in the life process together — every plant and animal species, the air, the water, and the soil — and we will survive or perish together.

Father Berry speaks of listening to the stories of the wind, the clover, and the seals. He describes how we can become sensitive to their needs and, in the process, to those parts of ourselves that we too often neglect. For me, discovering this clump of emerging fern fronds, or crosiers, was just one of those instances. I can give to the ferns what I endeavor to give my human friends and acquaintances — my respect and my care, which means not only paying careful attention to the composition and technical aspects of making this picture, but more especially being careful to leave the ferns and their habitat as I found them. And what are they giving me? An expression of symbiotic community living and sheer natural beauty! What more can I ask of them than that?

Yes, we belong here together. It is home for us all.

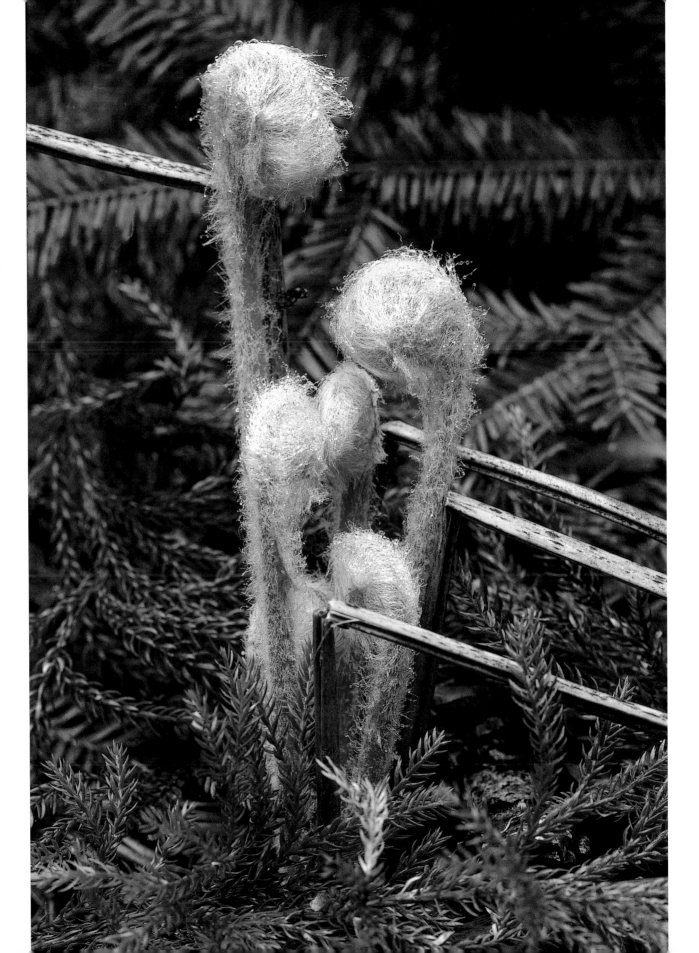

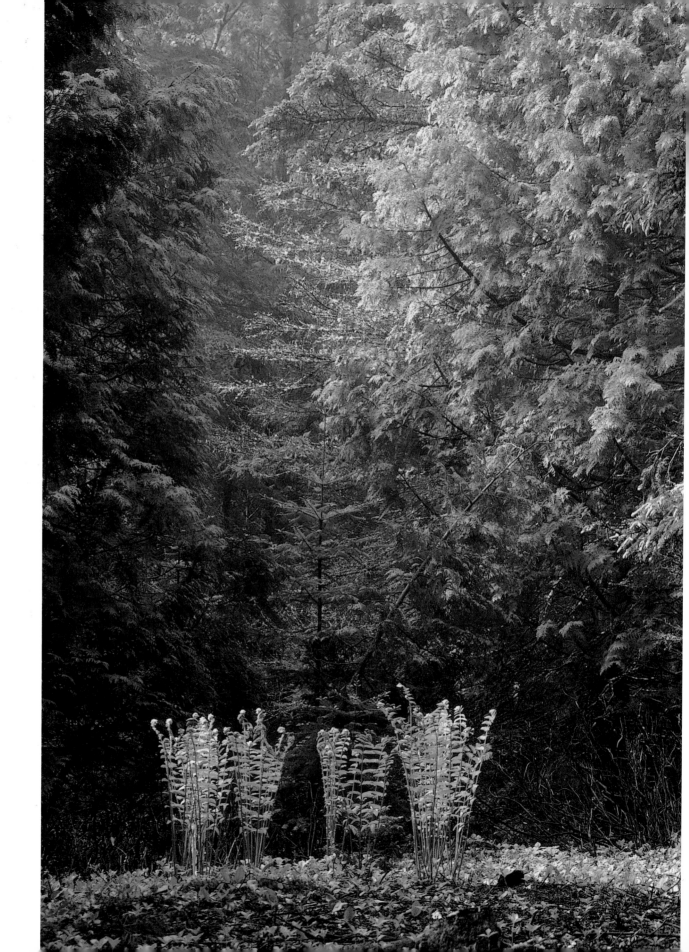

My garden grows wilder as I grow older. There's much less formality and restraint than there used to be, nothing planted in rows, and not a straight path to be found. I'm more tolerant of disorder as well, incorporating many beautiful "weeds" into flower beds simply by not pulling them out. I don't need or want to get anywhere as quickly or directly as I once did, either. Friends tell me I'm more laid-back than I used to be and, sure enough, the garden shows it.

This doesn't mean that I take less interest in the garden. I have more fun now than I used to, experimenting with ideas, both botanical and visual, and I'm much more inclined to put strangers together to see what happens, just as I do with guests at a dinner party. Also, if I like what's happening naturally in a certain spot, I simply proclaim it to be a garden, and put a bench there. Very labor saving and inexpensive!

Reflecting on my gardening makes me extremely aware of the influence or impact we all have on our surroundings, on situations and people — through both what we do and what we don't do. Gardens really are metaphors for how we live and what we consider important, and we learn the most about ourselves by observing what we have created.

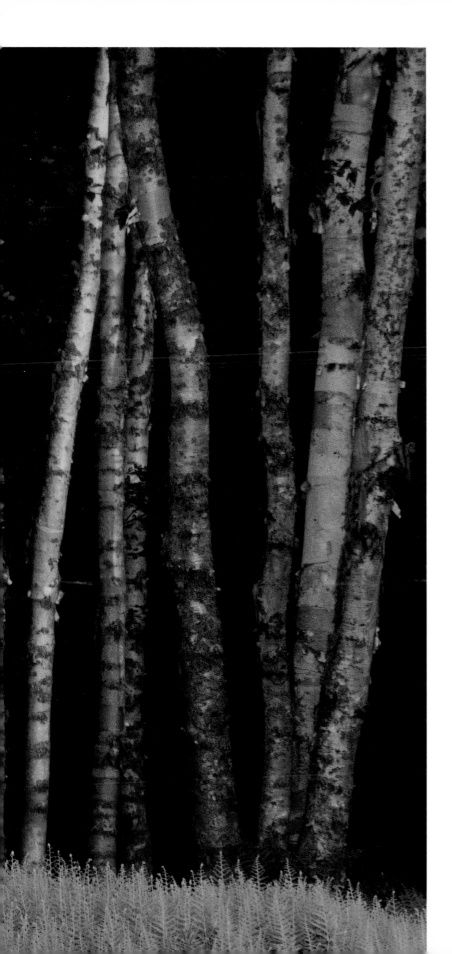

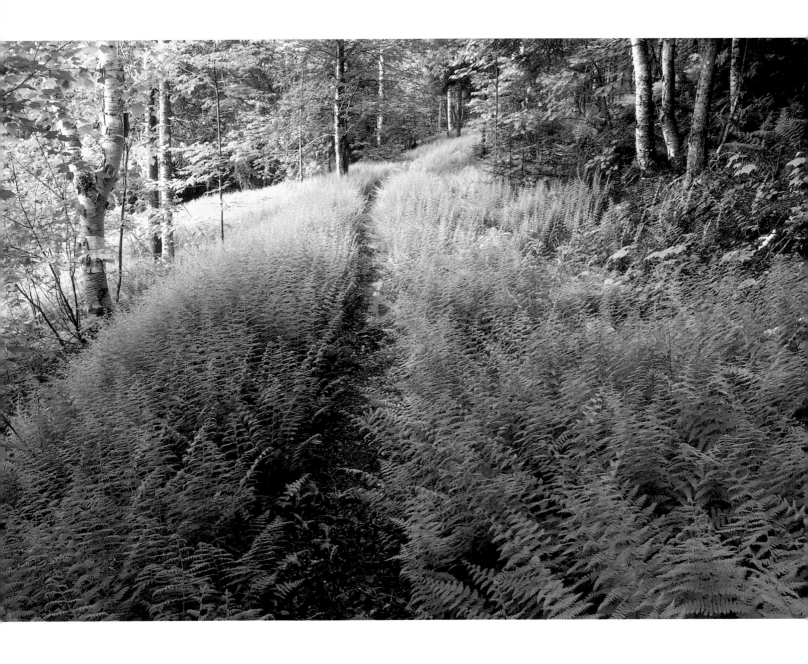

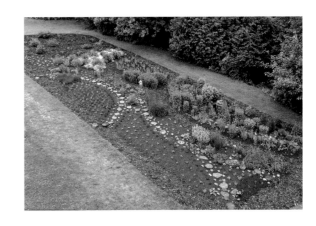

There are a lot of paths in my garden — well over a mile's (about two kilometers') worth. Wandering paths, of course! Straight lines won't do because they are too focused on a final destination, rather than on the process of getting there. The paths lead everywhere, or nowhere. One path may branch into three or four, and each of these branches, in turn, may develop byways, some that curve back to their route of origin. Where they go is always a matter of whimsy. (The small picture of the large garden bed was taken several years ago. Everything in it is carefully laid out. I'd never organize a garden so carefully today.)

The paths are an invitation to experience different biological communities and cultures. They provide easy access to hillside fields that are mowed every year in late autumn, but until then are a haven for nesting birds, small animals, and a variety of meadow plants. They often just take off into the unknown, always with the promise of discovering a secret place.

Sometimes, the easiest way to create a lovely garden is simply to mow paths through a field or patch of open ground — or what was formerly your lawn! Without doing another stitch of work, except for occasionally mowing them again, the paths will ensure you have a spring, summer, and fall filled with a succession of wildflowers and beautiful grasses that are easy to observe. Even in winter, if the snow isn't too deep, the paths will lure you out for a stroll.

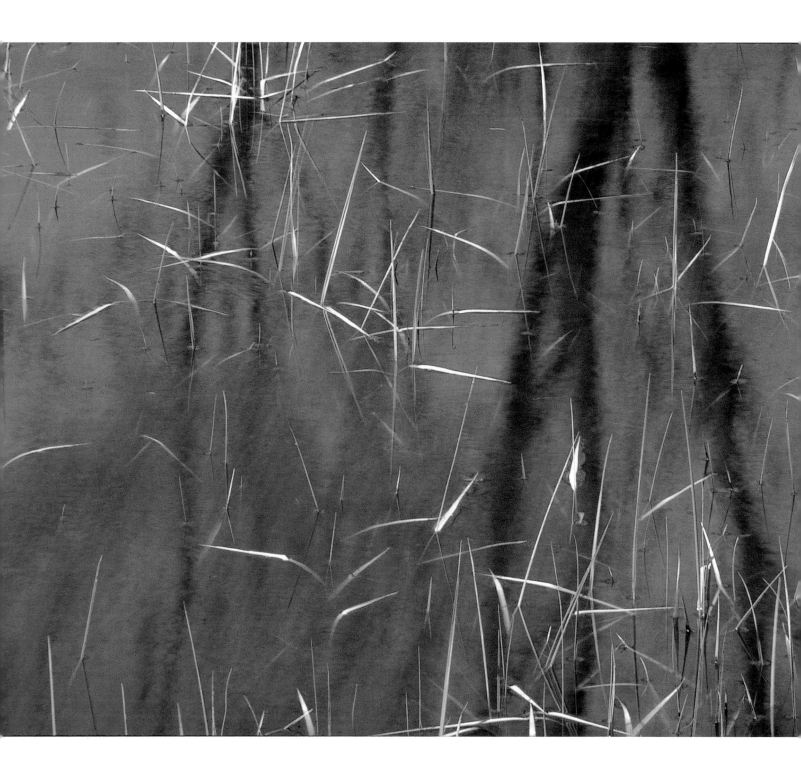

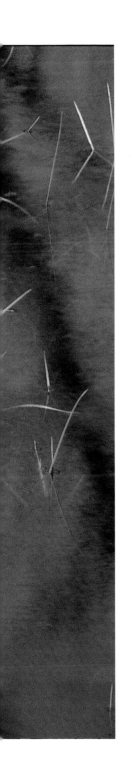

In addition to the enormous pleasure I derive from my panoramic view of the St. John River, I also enjoy frequent visits to other wet places — bogs filled with ferns and mosses, marshes near the river, and a brook that waxes and wanes with the rainfall and the seasons. Some very attractive wet places are temporary, such as this spring pool formed by a depression in a meadow.

One day I began to reflect on the large number of gardeners who add a pool, a pond, or even a small lake to their garden. Others may incorporate a natural stream, or perhaps circulate water through hidden hoses or pipes to tumble as a waterfall over rocks they have carefully added and arranged. I sometimes wonder if birdbaths are as much for the gardener as for the birds that splash in them or come to drink, because few symbols are more powerful and more common to all human cultures than water.

A friend told me recently of a dream she'd just experienced of water gushing up through the floor of every room in a big new house she was building. Afterward, we sat for the better part of an hour with a pot of tea discussing how these dream symbols, especially the water, seemed to express the new directions in her life.

Was I capturing dream symbols when I made this photograph, or was my response a purely visual one? Or both?

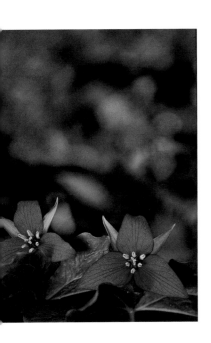

The purple or blue violet, *Viola cucullata*, is

the floral emblem for my home province of New Brunswick and, I'm happy to say, grows abundantly in dampish sections of meadows and very open woodland at Shamper's Bluff. When violets are blooming, usually beginning in early May and continuing for many weeks, hay-scented and sensitive ferns coming into their prime may provide a bit of cool shade that seems to encourage the violet clumps into vigorous development. I love poking around in an area below my house to find clumps with dozens of large, healthy blooms. A color like this is rare among spring-blooming plants.

Purple violets transplant easily into most gardens, but will continue to do well for only a year or two unless the gardener is able to approximate the plant's natural habitat, and doesn't just place them somewhere purely for show. Purple violets have to feel at home.

Red trilliums, or wake robins, are common in the woods of Shamper's Bluff, but only where deciduous trees dominate. Like most flowering plants that live on the forest floor, they require considerable light, which they receive before aspens, birches, maples, and other trees are in full leaf, in order to initiate their life cycle and flower. These blossoms are somewhat redder than most; they are normally a deep wine red color.

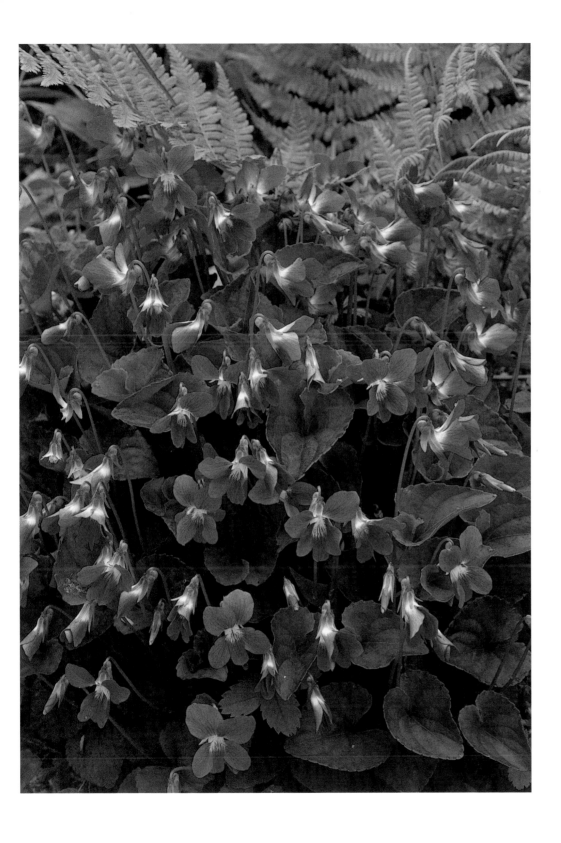

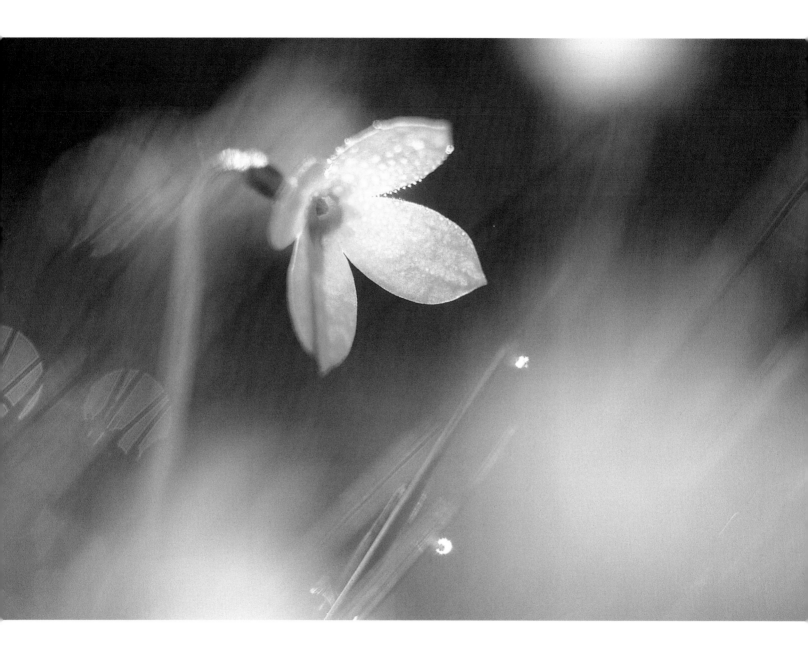

Children spend a lot of time rolling in the
grass, or lying flat on it, or creeping around on their hands
and knees. All of these positions are terrific for viewing
flowers, such as this tiny bluet. There's magic happening down
there in the grass. Then, of course, we grow up, and eventually
come to regard the height to which we grow as being sacred.

A friend of mine in her seventies, a very fine photographer
of flowers who had been hobbling around painfully for a
decade, recently had both knees replaced. I saw her the other day
lying in the dust of a farm road pointing her camera lens up at
the flowers growing along the verge. She was photographing
them from underneath. How long has it been since you looked
at a flower that way? If you have a plant on a windowsill or a
bouquet of flowers on your dining-room table, you can find the
magic just as easily now as you did when you were a child.

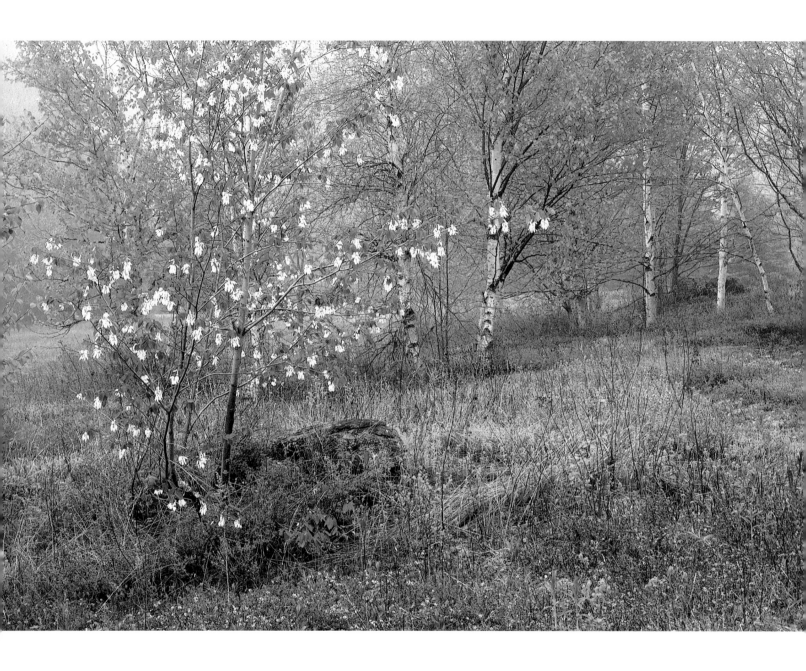

A hush pervades every part of my garden on damp, misty spring days, especially after a night of rain. I sense the stillness most of all in places that are largely wild, though I'm never quite sure why. Perhaps the random patterns of natural habitats induce a sense of quietness more readily than the often definite organization of domestic gardens. Perhaps in other weather conditions, such as brilliant sunshine, the strong visual contrasts between dark shadows and bright highlights rouse me to action, and I feel a need to be "doing something," even though nature herself is usually doing whatever needs to be done.

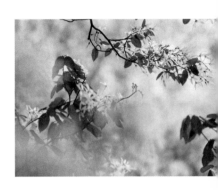

Days like these matter to me a great deal. Even in large formal gardens or tiny backyard patches, they slow me down. I pause longer in familiar places and appreciate fragrances and hues that otherwise I might never have noticed. As the sense of pressure or hurry drains away, I begin to feel reconnected with the natural world, and experience a strong, positive sense of self returning.

Such feelings are not nonsense; nor should the conditions that give rise to them be disparaged or ignored. Despite our vast urban and suburban habitats, which are primarily the home of only one species largely focused on itself, we are still profoundly dependent on and connected with the natural system. However, our self-induced blindness to it may be mitigated and our sense of wholeness regained when we enter a garden on a misty morning in spring to spend some quiet time with other living things.

When my sister and I were very young and heard our mother talking about rhododendron, we both thought that she was saying "road to Dendron," an exotic place to which we had never traveled. I can't remember when we came to understand what she was really saying, and realized that we had already experienced this wonderful place ourselves. To this day my sister and I prefer our original understanding, so every year I telephone her at the end of May or early June to tell her that the road to Dendron is in full bloom again, and she should come at once.

The large field below my house has huge patches of wild rhododendron — single, semi-double, and double flowers ranging from pale pink to deep cerise. I think of this large field as part of the garden: the plants require mowing every three years or so to ensure abundant annual blooms, and we create paths in the field that lead not only to the rhododendron, but in turn to purple violets, lupins, enormous spreads of wild blueberries, great swatches of hay-scented ferns, stands of bracken, and goldenrod. All the plants are native, but it takes some work to achieve continuing colorful displays and a good yield of blueberries.

My favorite times to wander along the road to Dendron are misty mornings and sunny evenings, when the moods induced by the weather are quite different, but equally intense.

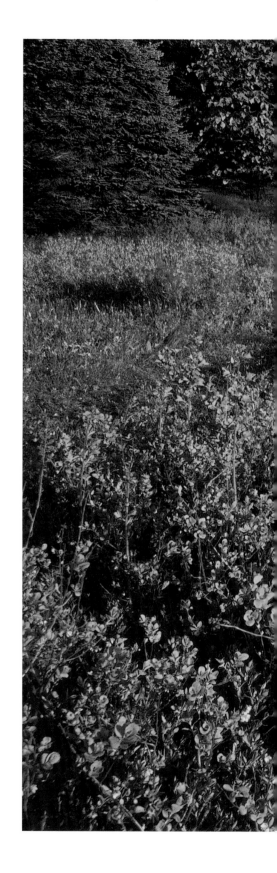

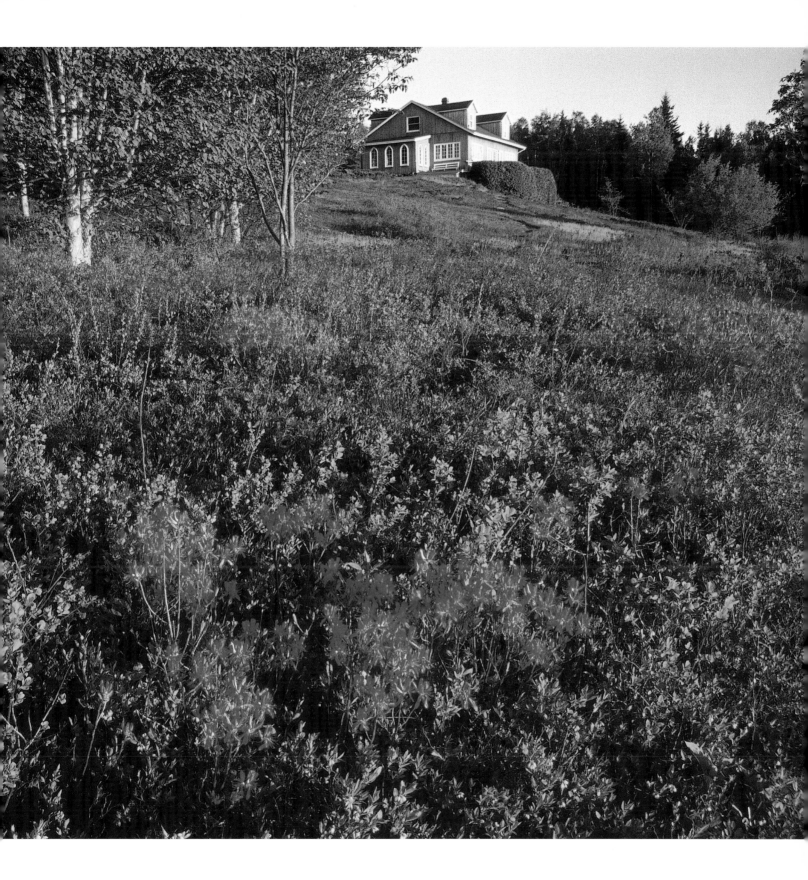

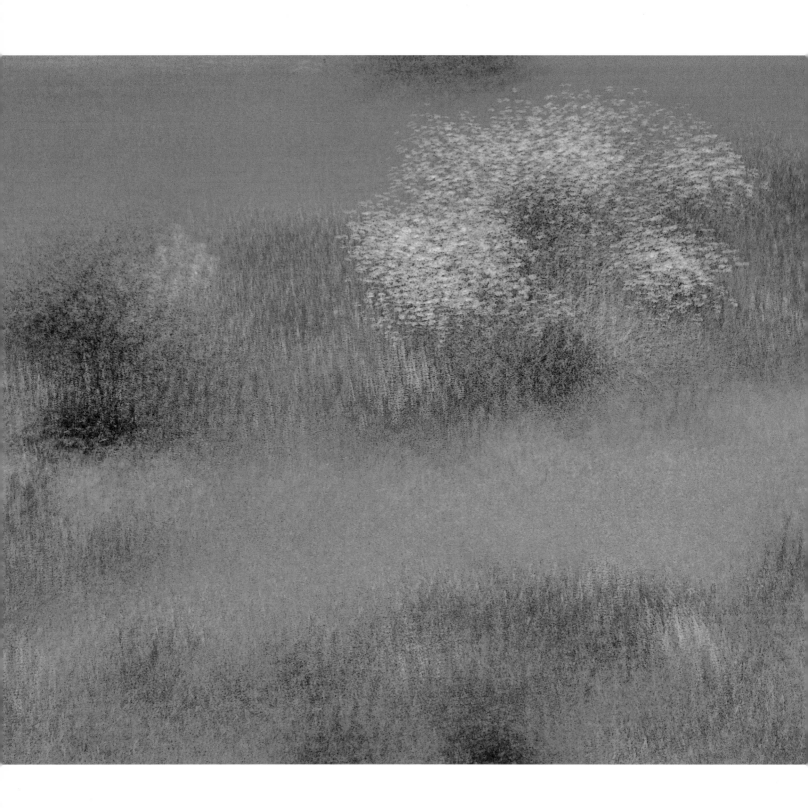

There are many times when a photographer or painter's sense of and feeling for a place can be expressed better with an impression than with a literal image. The sense or feeling is as important a reality as the place itself, and that's what the artist wants to evoke or express.

In spring, warm, delicate hues occur in a profusion unequaled at any other time of year. They have an enormous visual and psychological impact — arousing, stimulating, delighting, and refreshing us. Because the season's perfumes are often wafting on the breeze at the same time, also stimulating our brain, young people find it easy to fall in love, and everyone feels encouraged to tackle tasks that have long seemed too onerous. Birth and growth aren't just happening "out there" — they're also happening in us!

Can any of us really describe the feeling? Probably not with the rational, ordered left side of our brain, because that's not where the feeling comes from anyway. It originates in the mid-brain and its connection to the right cerebral cortex, which gardeners and artists employ when they dream and imagine what their creations may possibly — or impossibly — be like.

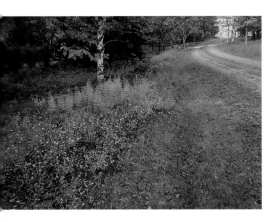

For years there had been a triangular patch along the upper part of my long driveway where everything and nothing seemed to grow. Oh, there was a bit of this and a little of that, but nothing seemed happy having to live in proximity to anything else. On various occasions I'd transplanted in some hay-scented ferns or removed bluebells that produced lots of leaves but never any flowers. I gave St. John's wort a try one year, but it took up with some strange grasses that didn't appeal to me, and after their cohabitation ended in failure, the ground seemed to remain strangely bare.

Now, as every gardener knows, gardening friends are worth their weight in flowers. They come to your rescue, frequently with plants, just when you need them. When I complained to my friend Joanne about this patch, she informed me that her son was about to dig up some drainage pipes near his house and, in the process, would certainly remove, or completely destroy, vast numbers of forget-me-nots. The next day Joanne arrived with three cartons of very healthy plants. When I had planted them all, I asked hopefully, "Are there any more of these?" "Thousands," she replied.

Then Joanne took over the project with a vengeance! She attacked my semi-wild garden with a whipper-snapper and a spade, added some *Rosa carolina* and other native perennials to the forget-me-nots, and tossed in seeds of dame's rocket and annual poppies.

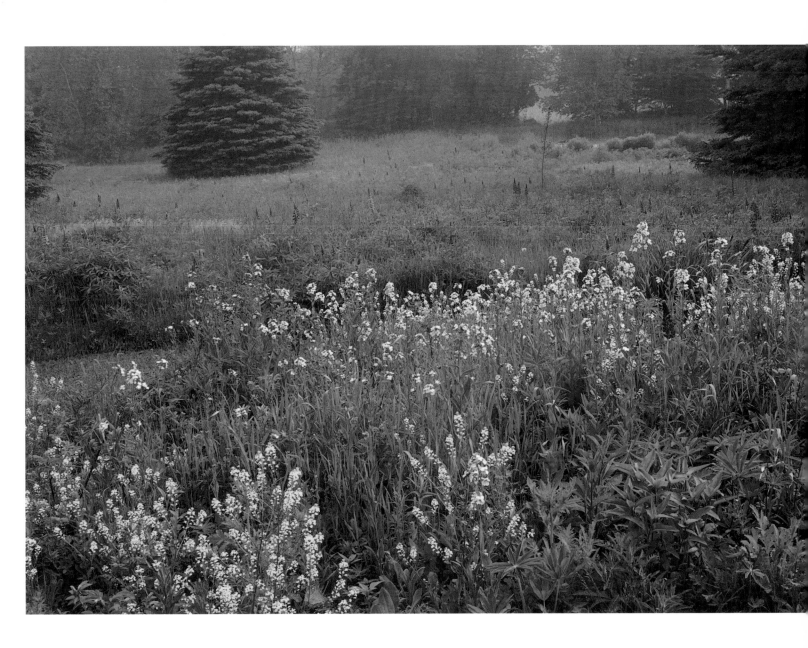

This enormous bilberry tree stands about

thirty feet (ten meters) from my front door. When May rolls around I can never refrain from making more photographs of it all dressed up and dancing. Come October, when the tree changes its party dress to glowing orange, I lose my restraint all over again.

Like Saskatoon berries, which grow on the prairies, bilberries are serviceberries (*Amelanchier* species), but the plants grow as trees, not as shrubs or bushes. Some people call them "sorbus," which sounds rather ponderous and heavy for blossoms that are delicate and just as delightful as the lovely dogwood that announces the full burst of spring in more temperate parts of the continent. Another name is "shad bush," because shad fish always begin their run in the rivers of eastern Canada and northeastern United States at the same time as bilberries begin to flower.

Bilberries hybridize freely, and although the blossoms of different varieties are very similar, the color of the emerging leaves may vary tremendously from tree to tree — ranging from restrained green to deep, rich reddish bronze. A tree that mixes reddish leaves with white blossoms appears, from a distance, as an explosion of delicate pink. The beauty rivals that of flowering crabapples, cherries, and other spring-flowering trees for which many people pay substantial amounts of money, while bilberry saplings are readily available from roadside ditches and verges.

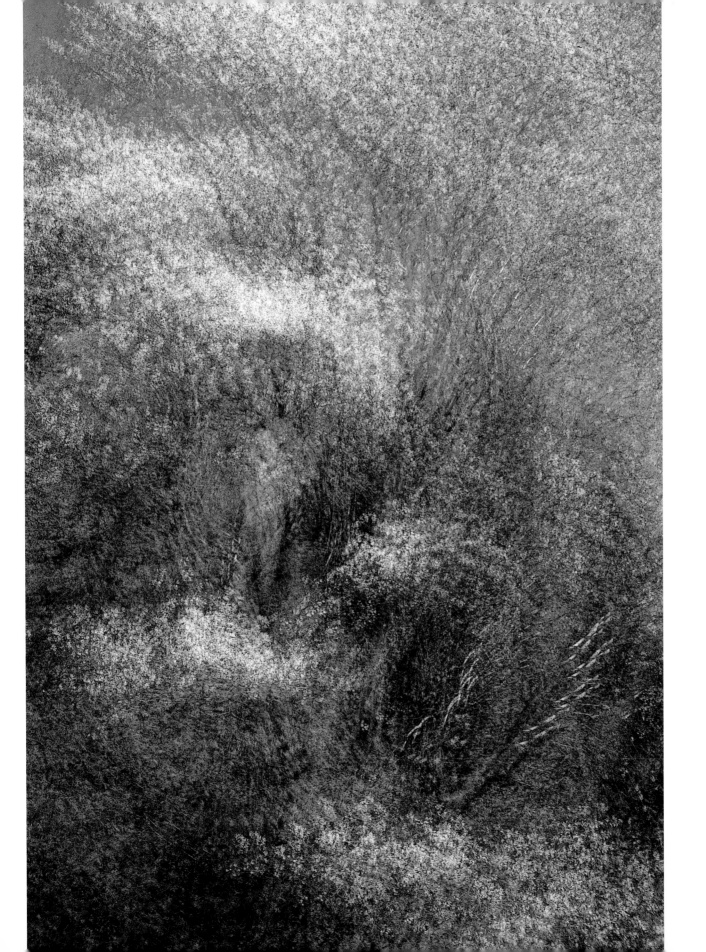

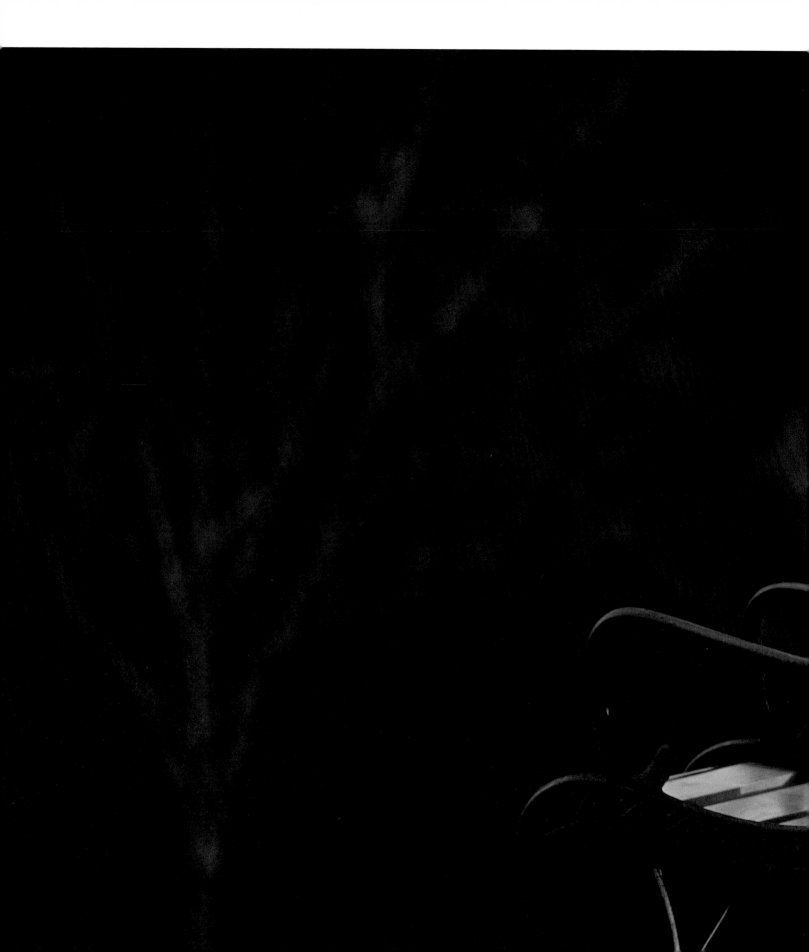

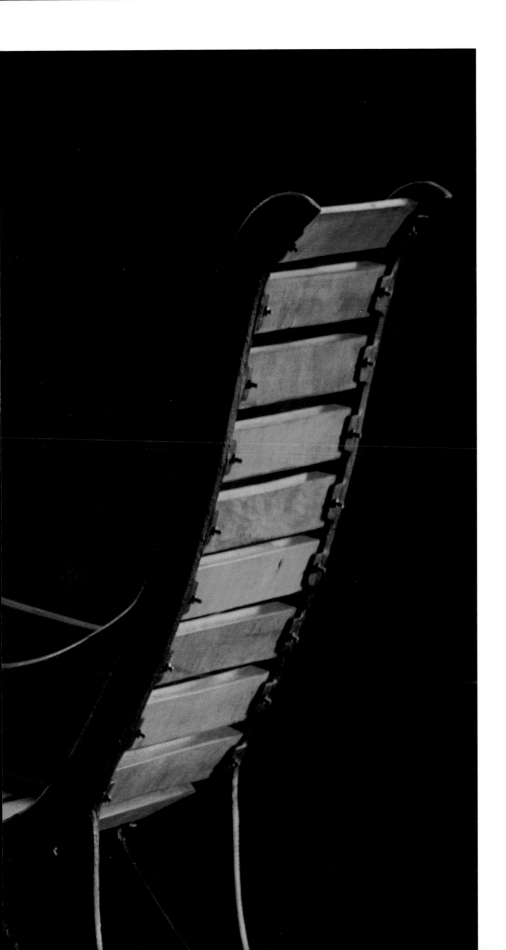

SUMMER

For some people, their garden is Eden. There they find the precious work that ushers them into eternity, where time seems to stand still and work is once again pleasure.

THOMAS MOORE, "Original Self"

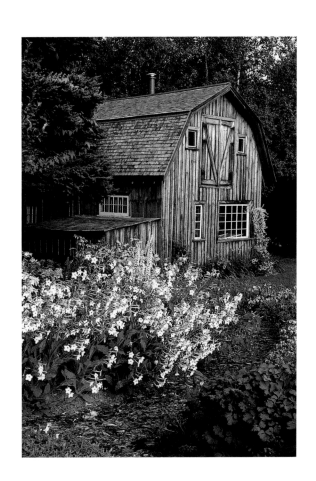

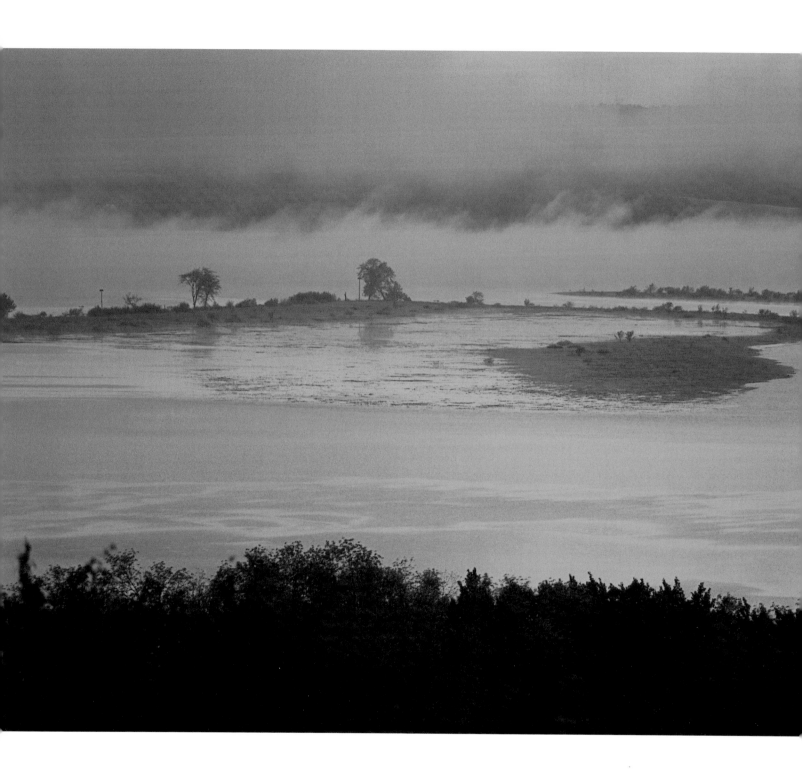

When the sun has not yet risen but the gentle pink of the morning sky colors the water and river mists below my house, I often take my wake-up coffee to a bench on the front deck. In the hush broken only by the singing and calling of birds, I feel that I am living in the Heaven I imagined as a child. Of course, it's a matter of perception. Some people I know hardly give the view a second glance, and I sometimes wonder if they would appreciate Heaven should they ever be fortunate enough to get there.

When the sun goes to rest below the western horizon, often bouncing its remnant gold, orange, and red rays off lingering clouds to ripple along river currents, I carry a glass of wine to the same bench. There, in the sweet, lingering quiet, punctuated occasionally by the harrumphing of green frogs, I watch Heaven fading in the dying light. Of course, this is also a matter of perception. Even in the darkest of nights a few highlights remain to guide my imagination and, as I peer into the uneven blackness, I am reminded that it's not really the eye that does the seeing, it's the soul.

Let's imagine.

Let's suppose that on this particular morning the water dreamed of my coming, and that the mist deliberately softened the colors of dawn to complement the delicacy of the grasses and other aquatic plants. Let's assign conscious intentions to what we've been taught are unconscious things. And then, let's compare these seemingly ridiculous notions with other nonsensical ones.

Once it was unreasonable to imagine that Earth revolved around the sun; in fact, people were executed for believing this heresy. And, for a very, very long time, we thought we lived on a flat planet, and that sailors risked being carried helplessly over the great waterfall at the edge of the sea. Until very recently, we conceived of only one universe — vast beyond all comprehension, but one, nonetheless. Now quantum physicists are postulating a multiverse, parallel universes in space and time, regretting certainly that our five senses do not pick them up. Maybe our senses will evolve, just as our ability to perceive new colors has evolved so incredibly during the past twenty-five hundred years. It's hard to believe now that Aristotle saw only a "three-colored rainbow."

So maybe I shouldn't be too concerned about what is reasonable. That's not what gardening is all about.

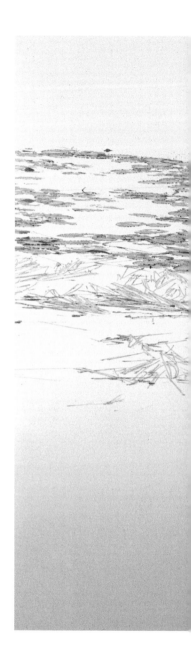

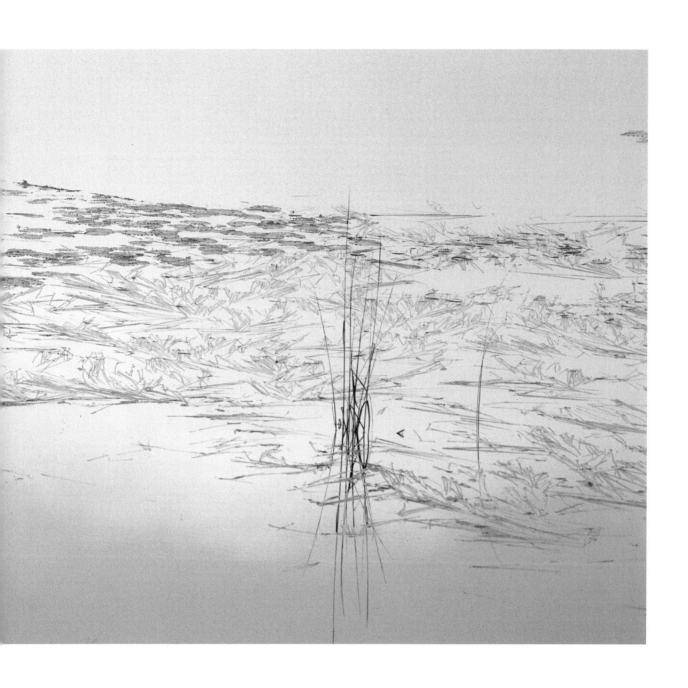

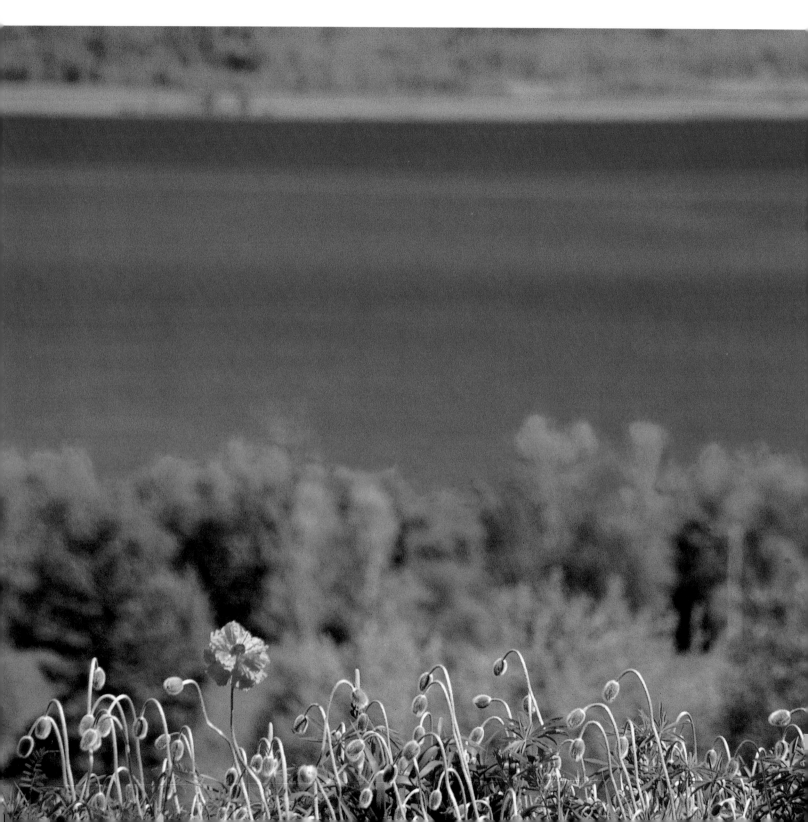

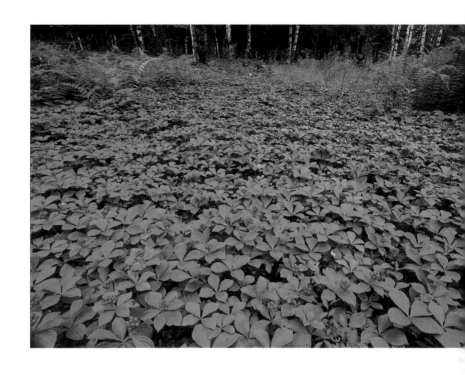

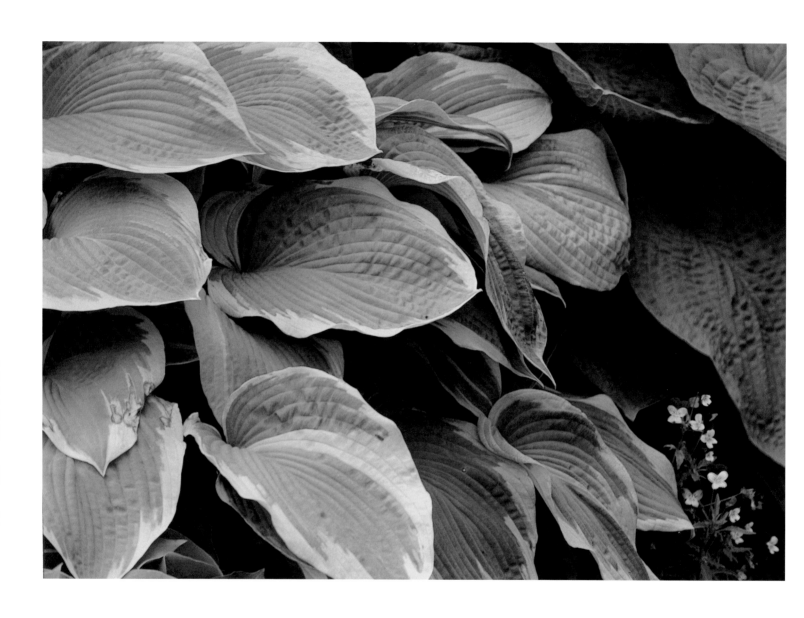

By early summer the hosta plants that are pictured on page 24 had filled every last bit of their bed, except for one tiny space. Here a little pansy plant, also known as a Johnny-jump-up, found its niche, or "jumped up."

The hostas sometimes remind me of the mythological tale of the four fire-breathing dragons guarding the temple — the small open space. If you were trying to gain access to the temple, you would perceive the dragons as a threat. If you managed to get by them and planted yourself in the temple, however, you would then perceive them as your protectors. And you could blossom, rather than struggle.

Was this another example of David challenging Goliath? Or, was it a group of secure individuals, a healthy community allowing for diversity in its midst?

From Johnny's point of view, and mine too, nothing was occupying the space, so why not make use of it? Besides, the shade of the huge hosta leaves discouraged competitive weeds, kept the soil moist on even the hottest days, and protected against the wind. It was a very good place for Johnny to live.

And from the purely aesthetic perspective, the clump of tiny pansy blossoms functions as a striking accent, a colorful jewel in the tapestry of green and yellow leaves and black shadows.

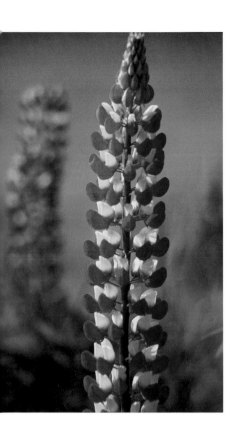

Depending on which way I look from my house from mid-June to mid-July, I can see one lupin blossom or about two million. The lupins have been growing here for a long time. They escaped from the gardens of early settlers, and have naturalized to become so abundant in this region that many people think of them as the unofficial floral emblem of Canada's three Maritime provinces.

Along the verges of major highways and secondary roads, the original colors — blue, pink, and white — are sometimes mixed with a much wider range of vibrant hues and bicolors, because somebody with an eye for beauty tossed a package or two of hybrid Russell lupins into the mix. After a few years the rainbow colors revert to the original three, except that parts of the individual florets on each floral column often echo one or more of the brilliant varieties, so following a path through a field of blues and purples soon becomes an exciting challenge in discovering the many secret hues.

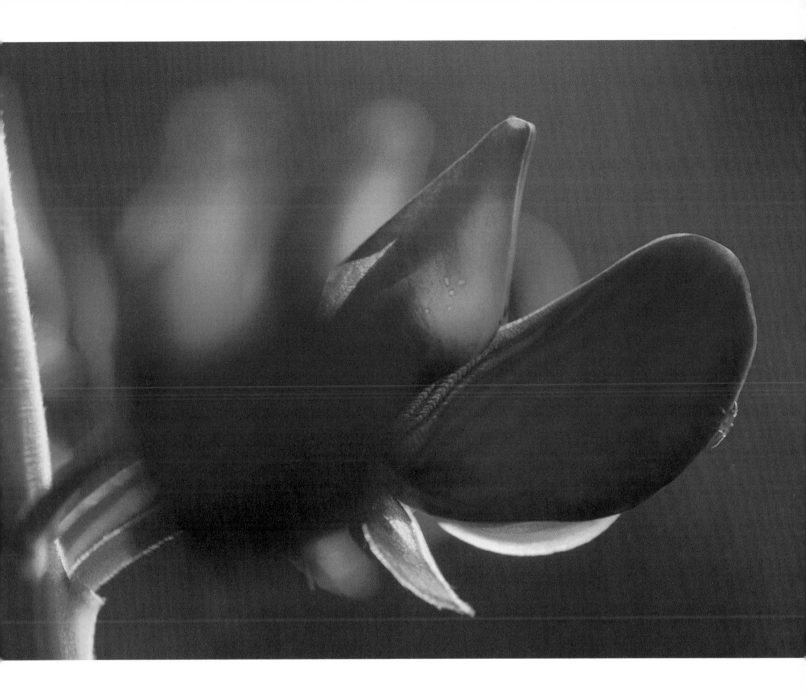

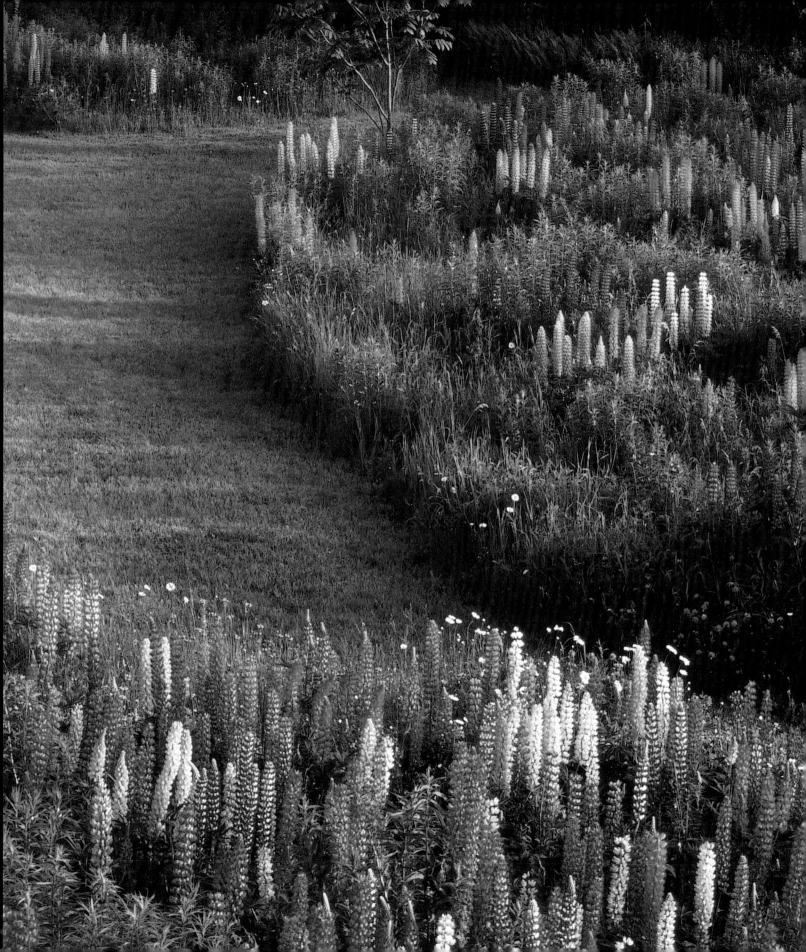

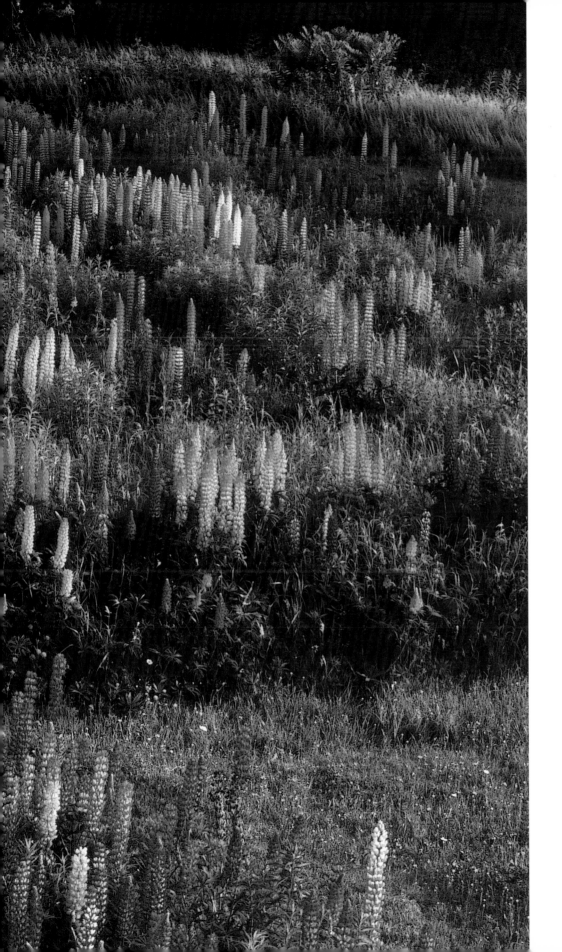

The importance of beauty to our lives

requires no explanation, and we never need to explain our reasons or apologize for actively seeking it out. My mother taught me that without ever putting it into words, and in the process she gave me life a second time.

Visual beauty, heart-stopping beauty, gently soothing beauty surrounds us every day of our lives, everywhere — a dandelion blossom emerging from a crack in the pavement, a cloud forming or dissipating in a deep blue sky, or the grain structure of a piece of lumber. We can be aware of it, enriched by it, even healed by it. Or not. The same is true for the beauty of sound and music. Although we are quick to hear noise, especially the screeching of tires, or the roar of a jet, we may be much slower to tune into the whisper of wind blowing through grasses, or the pings and plunks of raindrops splattering on our living-room window. We may be slower yet to admit our interest and delight in such things.

However, when we become aware of the beauty of water streaming down our windowpanes, chances are that even without trying we will sensitize others to the beauty around them and help to enrich their daily lives immeasurably.

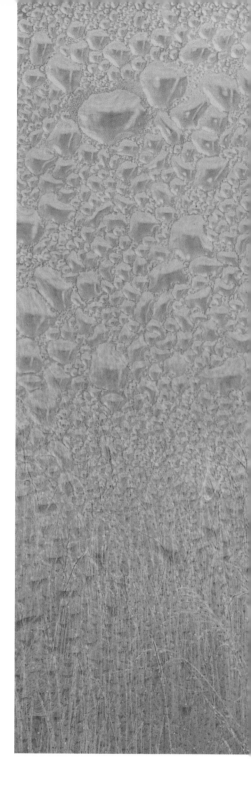

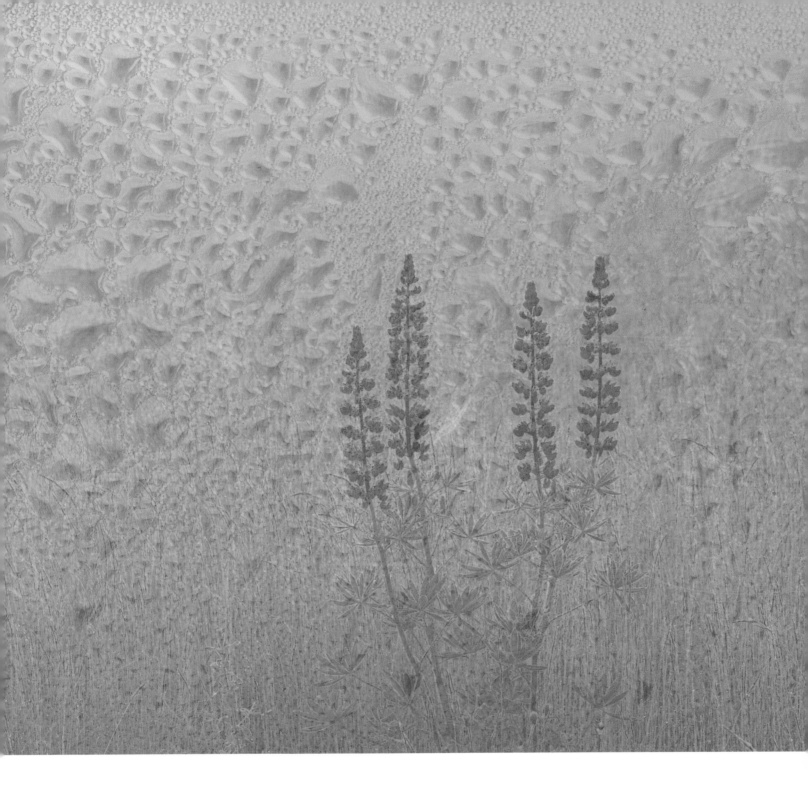

When we're down on our hands and knees pulling weeds or planting bulbs, we are forever observing little things, like this spider, and having thoughts about its life that, invariably, relate to our own. By keeping us in touch with natural things, gardening always helps to keep us in touch with ourselves. Because nature or creation is the universal scripture, neither shaped nor limited by particular cultures and religions, its relevance is fundamental for all people and all things. The little spider hanging among wild cucumber blossoms in a morning mist is one small verse in a very large text.

As this spider prepares for lunch — going to market, as it were, by spinning a web to catch a juicy insect — it is supremely confident about its future prospects. It is doing what it was genetically encoded to do. The spider doesn't worry about eating on time. It will dine when the meal arrives. In many ways, it might be good for us to get back to that way of thinking — daring to hang by a thread, which exposes us to the world, instead of having a constant obsession about security, which means focusing on our fears and apprehensions.

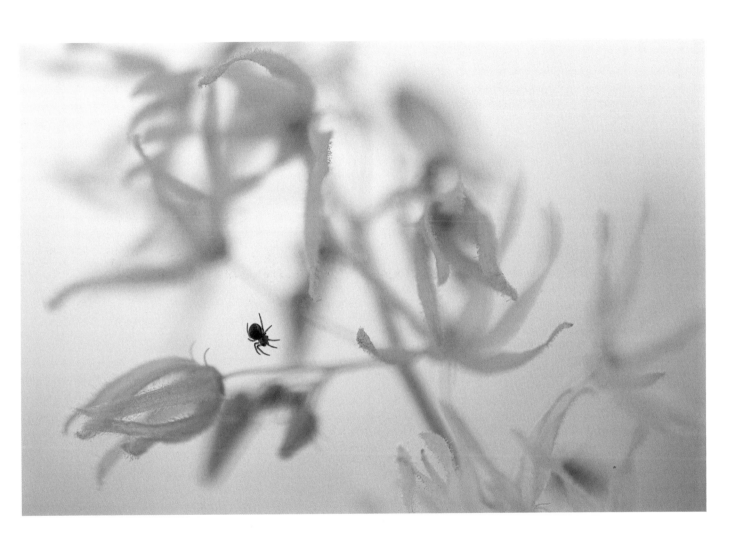

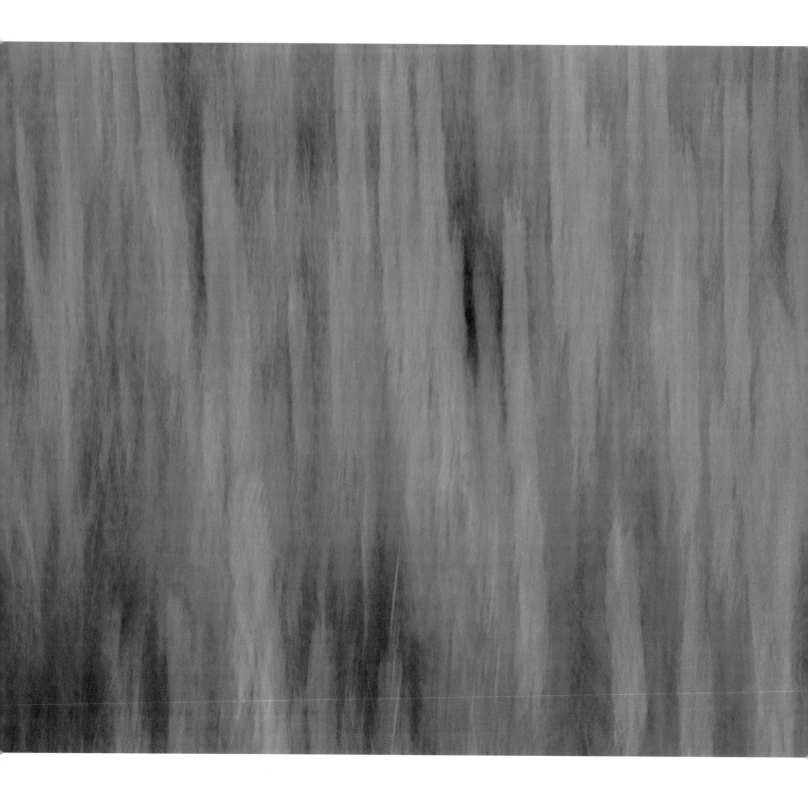

In many areas of southern Canada and the northern United States, purple loosestrife is an exotic plant that, lacking natural competitors, has come to dominate many damp habitats, obliterating native species. Campaigns to eliminate it are legion, even in communities where it has reached an equilibrium and has not increased in many years, which is true around here. There seems to be neither more nor less loosestrife than there was when I was a child.

Although loosestrife is a very beautiful flower, it can threaten an entire ecosystem. However, several other exotic species, equally widespread, oppressive, and damaging — but less beautiful — are allowed to go unchecked. Nobody seems even to notice them.

With plants, and with life in general, we often mount campaigns against beautiful things, but do nothing about ugliness. Dandelions are another example. We've been taught that they are ugly — in order to sell herbicides. People rarely talk about how nutritious the green leaves are, or about their medicinal value, or about the cheeriness they bring to a spring meadow. Why not take the money we spend annually to fight dandelions and, instead, use it to eliminate utility poles and transformers planted in front of beautiful cathedrals and churches or along magnificent stretches of highway?

It's something of a conundrum. Meanwhile, I am enjoying purple loosestrife pirouetting in roadside ditches.

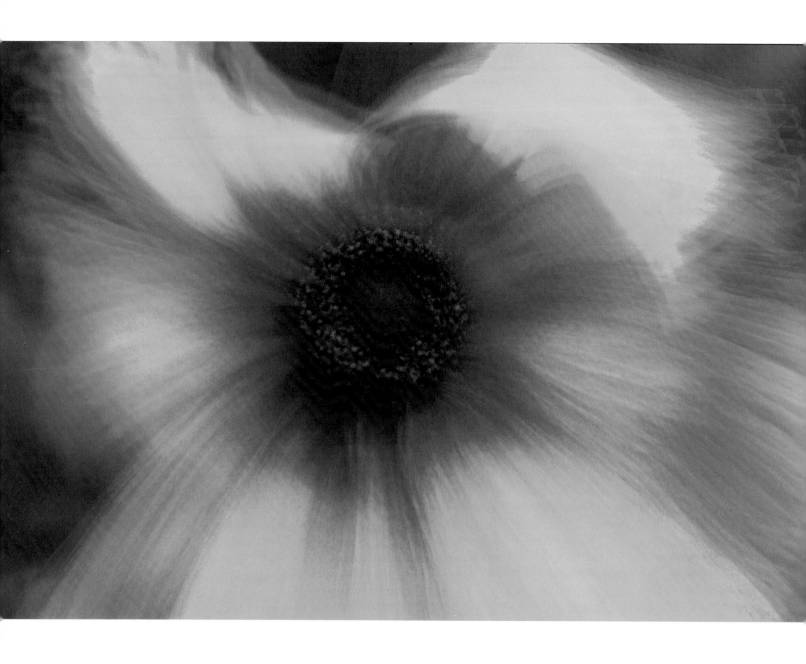

Flowers growing out of doors spend a lot of time blowing in the wind. With most flowers it doesn't take much wind; even a hint of breeze seems to set them dancing. Many photographers find this unacceptable and will expend enormous amounts of energy, time, and technique trying to make them stand still. They'll use fast shutter speeds and flash to arrest motion, erect shelters to block the wind, or simply exercise enormous patience, waiting for even a brief pause in a strong wind.

Being tossed around is an essential part of many flowers' existence, however, and many plants owe their lives to wind, which carries pollen from flower to flower. No wind, no fertilization, no descendents. Insects can't do it all. So I think it's fine to show flowers shimmering, tossing, dancing, and bending. Most of them are built to do just that, and they do it very successfully, unless the wind velocity is extreme.

Like photographers who always try to make their flower pictures "sharp" and "in focus," we often try to make people and things fit preconceived modes of existence or behavior. Often, as with photographing flowers, we are more in favor of constraint than freedom, more disposed to rules than guidelines, more appreciative of similarities than differences. I sometimes wonder what kind of gardener, or photographer, might need limits and boundaries. Maybe just beginners, but even for them I'm not sure.

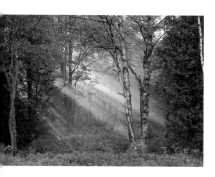

This is a paradox that repeats in our lives: having to give up one thing in order to have another. Very seldom do we experience what both sides of our brain want to do, without the intentions of one side interfering with the desires of the other.

On this ethereal morning I was torn between wanting to experience the peace of the moment and wanting to record the incredible, fleeting beauty of sun and mist. By making the pictures, I created a visual cue with which to stimulate my feelings again and again. However, I also had to give up something — pure, uncluttered enjoyment — because the composition and exposure decisions I had to make required that I engage my left brain.

Life frequently calls upon us to make choices — especially, it seems, in the presence of unsurpassed beauty — as the practical perspective confronts the aesthetic and spiritual one. Balancing the two effectively can sometimes be difficult.

How do we choose? I endeavor to see the opposing forces as complementary. Gardening is all about feeling, for example, but thinking is required in order for us to feel good about our gardens. Art of any kind necessarily depends on the left-brain concentration of craft that is necessary to produce the desired right-brain response. And it is in the feeling, not in the facts, that we find meaning.

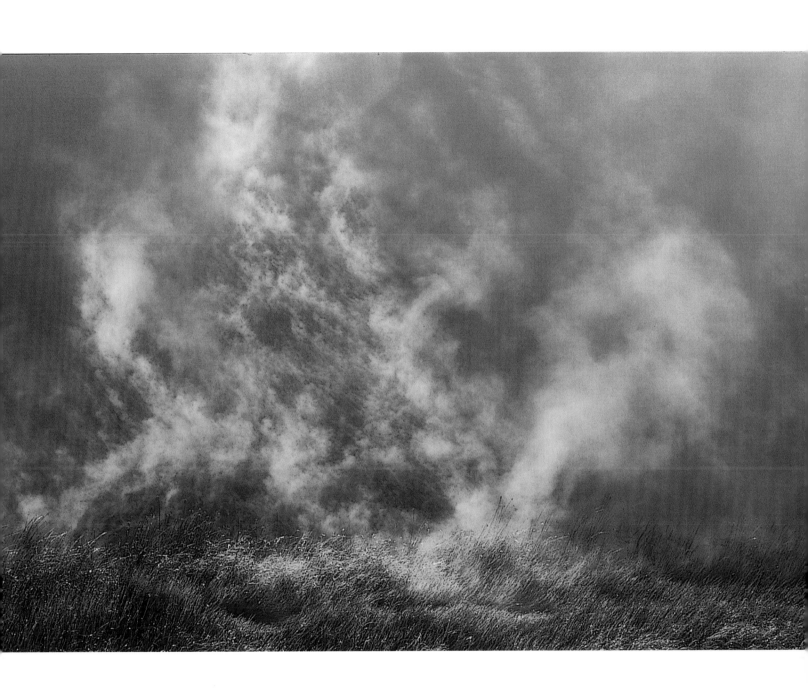

One sunny afternoon while I was watching robins pulling earthworms from the soil after a heavy shower, a big red fox came strolling up the center of my driveway and cut across the grassy patch where they were so busily engaged. As it started down one of the paths that wander through the field, the fox paused, listened, and pounced! I couldn't quite see, but a field mouse may have bit the dust. Having apparently scored once, the fox continued to sniff slowly along the path.

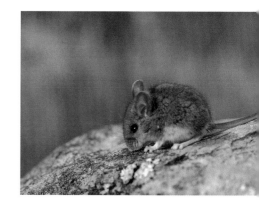

Then a raccoon came humping out of the woods in a big hurry, startling a bobolink sitting on a tall blade of timothy grass as it raced by. The bobolink crossed the field in its typical undulating flight pattern and settled on a thistle, where I had noticed a goldfinch picking at seed fluff only moments before. A kestrel, also looking for a mouse, paid the raccoon no attention whatever.

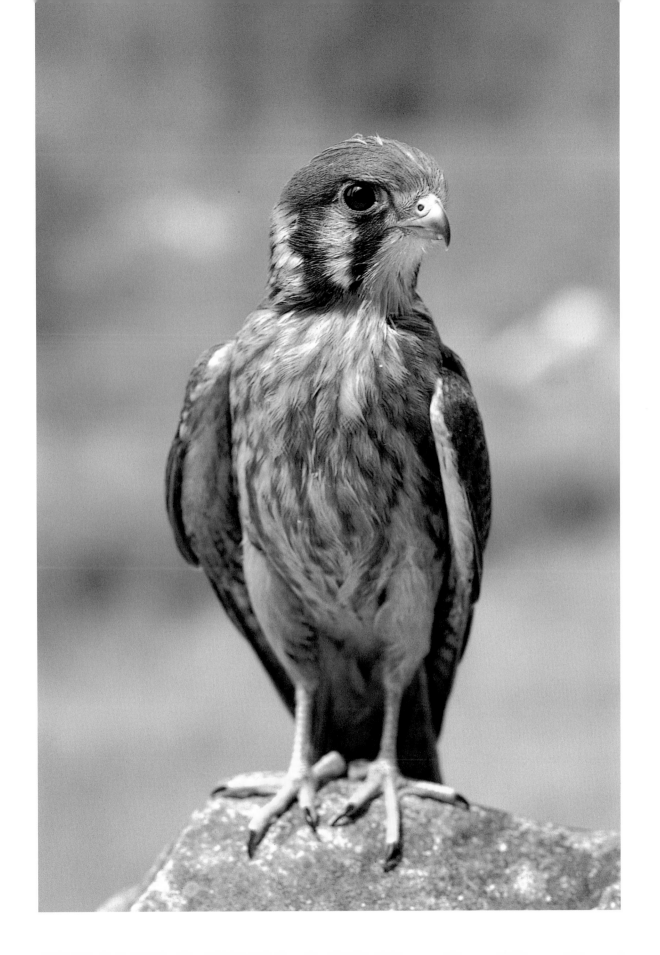

There are many busy spiders in my gardens and the surrounding fields, and on most clear mornings everything in the gardens and fields, including spiders' webs, is studded with dewdrops. The experience of one such morning always makes me eager for the next one.

When we put a label on anything, we restrict or diminish our ability to see the full range of its faces. So sometimes I challenge myself to photograph a lawn chair, a piece of kitchen foil, or a spider's web without ever revealing what it is — without showing its label. From a visual point of view, my aim is to keep my "seeing" fresh, to avoid looking at or photographing anything in consistently predictable or stereotypical ways. Although referring to webs as "strings of pearls" may seem apt, when we realize that this descriptive analogy, too, is a label, we'll keep on crawling through our gardens, lying on our backs under shrubs, tilting our heads this way and that, all in order to experience these incredible constructions more fully.

One morning four little girls from the neighborhood visited me. They were all between five and eight years of age, with energy to burn. No sooner had they announced their visit than the quartet raced down one of the long paths that leads into the sloping field in front of my house, then split off, one after the other, as side paths appeared. Within moments the leader disappeared into the woods, another was jumping up and down beside a chokecherry bush trying to grab a fistful of berries, a third clambered over a large granite rock, while the fourth was busily engaged in picking a bouquet of daisies. Each seemed to have her own spontaneous agenda, which now and then coincided with all the others, and they would commence a group activity without anyone having even suggested it.

At one point the girls were singing and dancing frenetically around a big pot of red geraniums sitting behind my house, all four falling down over and over again only to rise once more and charge back into the game. Just as I deduced that they must be playing ring-around-the-rosy, first one, then another, then all four started spinning like a top as they circled around the pot. To me they resembled four feverishly speeded-up planets, each spinning erratically on her axis around a red sun. After they had left, I went out to replicate what they had been doing and discover what they may have seen while they were revolving around the sun.

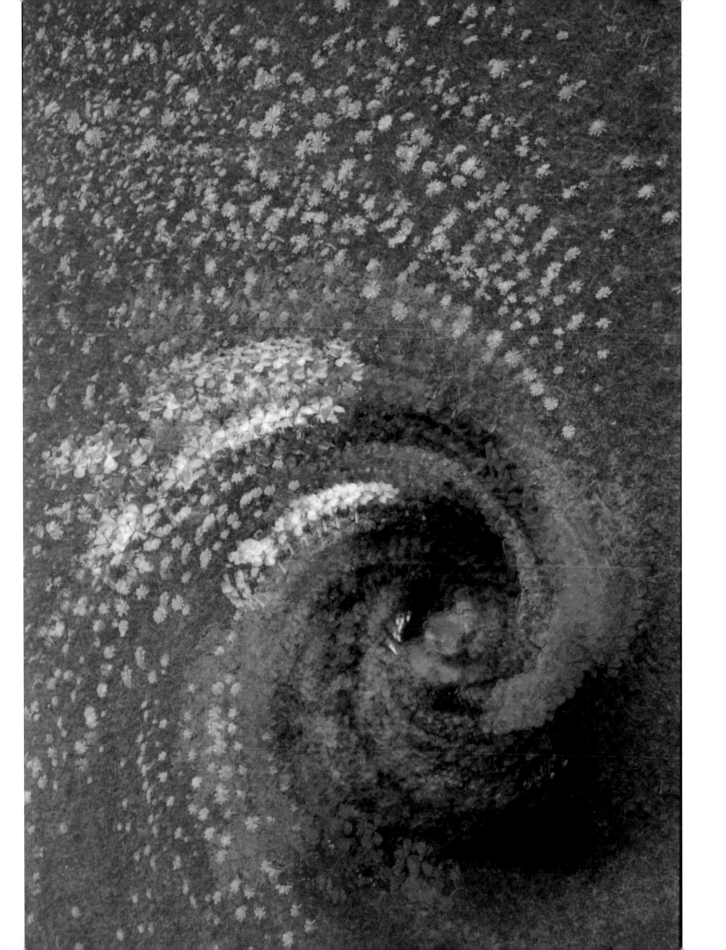

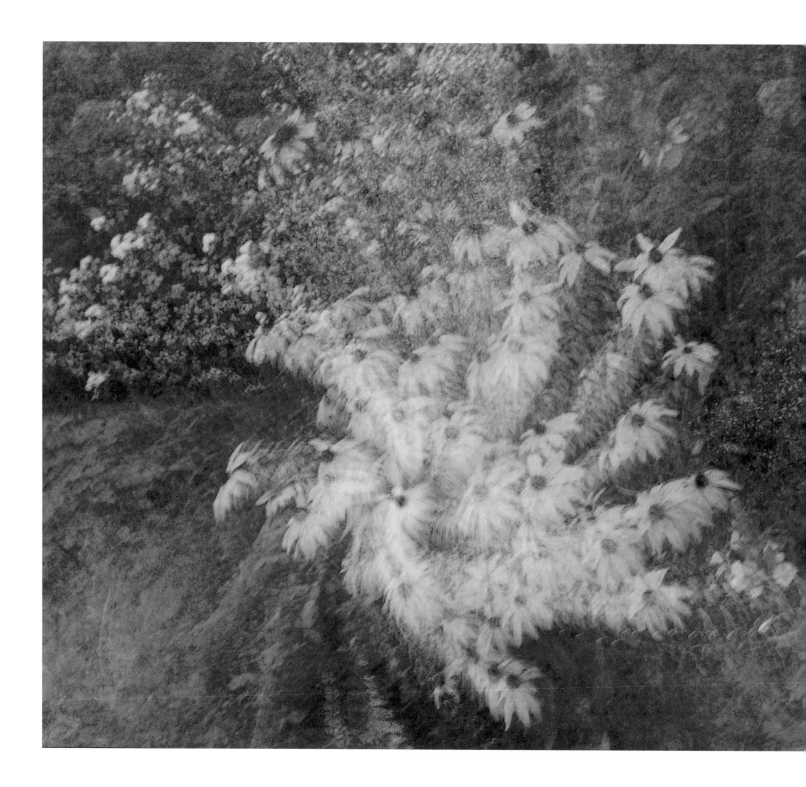

Gardening always requires a degree of imagination. When it comes to vegetables, however, you will have to restrict your imagination. You can't play around with the design of a vegetable garden, for example, if you have to deliver several tons of tomatoes to the warehouse by the end of the month. Gardening with flowers around your home is quite another matter. You have only yourself to please, and should allow your imagination free rein.

Imagining something is not the same as doing it, but it's a terrific place to begin. You'll only have climbing roses or clematis tumbling down from your balcony if you come up with the nonsensical idea of planting climbers up in the air instead of down in the ground.

It's one thing to garden "with" your imagination, but another to garden "in" your imagination. Photographers and painters do it all the time. It's always satisfying to have good documents of your garden, but equally to have flowers leaping and whirling and dancing in your mind, on film, or on a canvas. Where did the "Waltz of the Flowers" come from, after all? And *Fantasia*, too? I believe we should consider all these imaginary images as documentary expressions of feelings, such as delight, hope, merriment, wonder, and joy!

Last year on this sloping hillside I scattered a lot of
annual seeds — four kinds of poppies, magenta lychnis,
English wallflowers, lots of bachelor's buttons or cornflowers,
and a few others species — all of which bloomed nicely.
Among them were a few native ox-eye daisies, brown-eyed
Susans, gaillardia, and sweet William, all biennials, and a rose
bush or two. This year, both the annuals and biennials have
outdone themselves. Before I even considered tossing new
seeds into the ground during the very cold, late spring, the
seeds that had lain all winter in this garden had begun to
germinate. All I've had to do since is pull some "weeds" and
make pictures of everything.

In nature, but only rarely in gardens, everything — plants
and animals — seeds itself and life goes on as abundantly as
the habitat permits. Why, then, do gardeners have to sow seeds
every spring? Why don't the plants just come up and save us
all that bother?

Usually, it's because we try to grow plants that are not
native to the environment. As I became more observant, I
noticed that an occasional non-native annual species was
replanting itself very nicely. Every such species went on my
"Yes!" list. Also, I asked other gardeners what they were
having good luck with. This year my attention paid off.

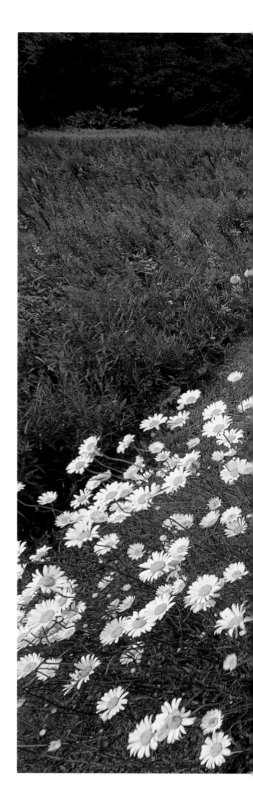

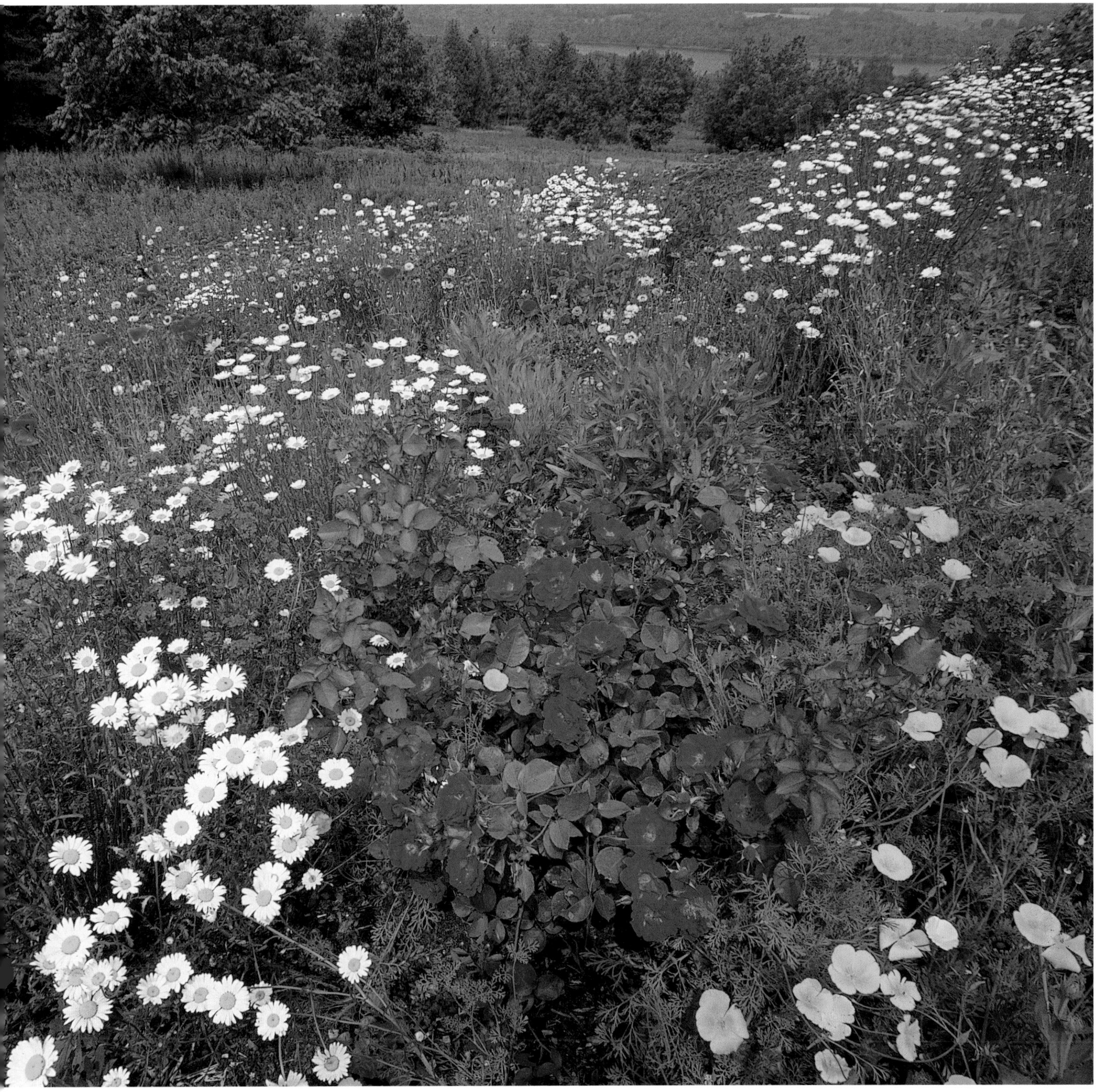

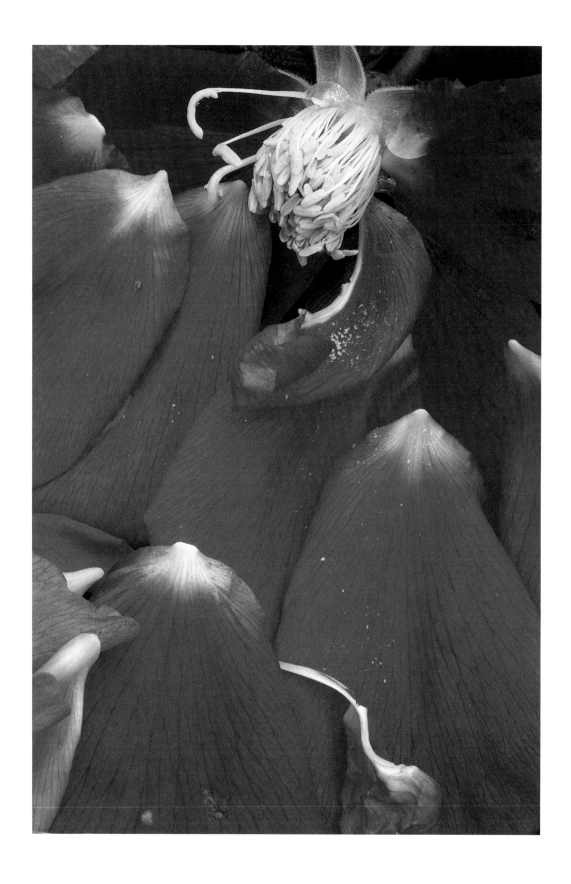

In May 1783 about 150 United Empire Loyalists, having been evicted from their homes in Connecticut and Long Island, New York, sailed up the St. John River as far as Belleisle Bay. Three men rowed ashore and, after scouting the area, suggested they all sail around the tip of what is now called Shamper's Bluff, where they disembarked in what became Portage Creek, and later, Kingston Creek. One of those men, only eighteen at the time, was buried sixty-three years later on a high point of land overlooking the bay. This spot, probably an open field at the time, is now on the edge of the woods about fifty feet (fifteen meters) from my front door. Three sons, who predeceased him, and his wife are buried beside him. There are other people buried here as well, the most recent being my aunt, who died in 1998.

In addition to these burial sites, there is a healthy sugar maple in a field near my house with a small engraved stone under it, both placed in memory of a woman from California by her fellow participants in a photographic workshop held a few years ago. Soon another memorial will be created for a second woman, also deeply loved by the members of the workshop that she attended. Also, one day when I was by myself, I planted a basswood tree as a living memorial to my mother, who loved flowers, and trees, and birds, and dewdrops on spiders' webs, and who might have remarked on the fragrance of the rose from which these petals have fallen.

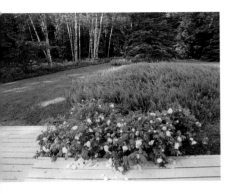

Over a year before I made the photograph of snow and grass on page 166, I photographed these rose and delphinium petals, which a visiting friend had spread out on a screen to dry for potpourri. Despite the difference of subject matter, you'll immediately notice the similarity in the way I approached both situations.

When it comes to planning both gardens and photographs, I find it useful, sometimes very instructive, to ask why I'm repeating myself. I'm not automatically against repetition, because it can be both a good learning tool and an important design element. Rhythm, for instance, is a color, tone, or note repeated at regular or predictable intervals, giving structure and order to both visual and musical compositions. However, pure repetition often indicates an unconscious development. For example, it may be a warning that I'm getting stuck in a rut. Or, conversely, it may signal a new trend in myself, of which I should become consciously aware.

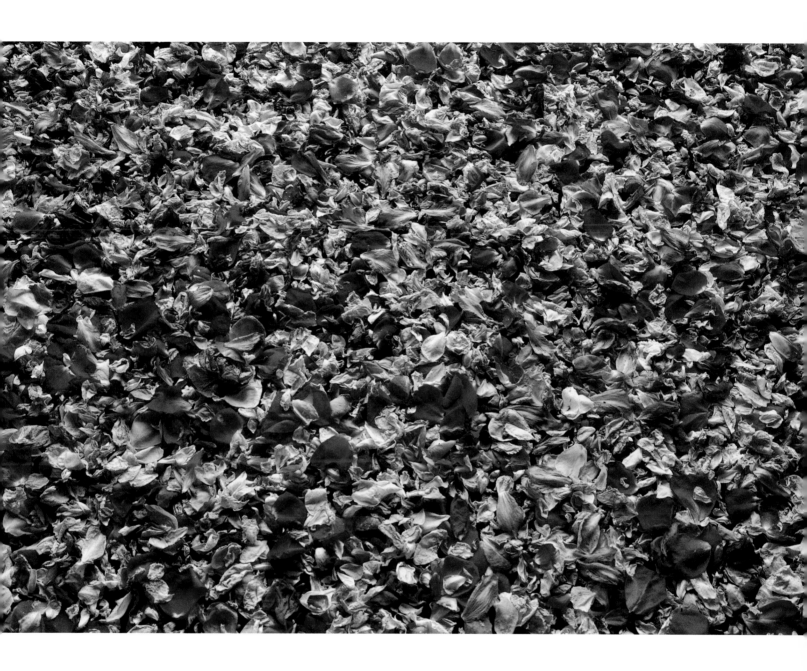

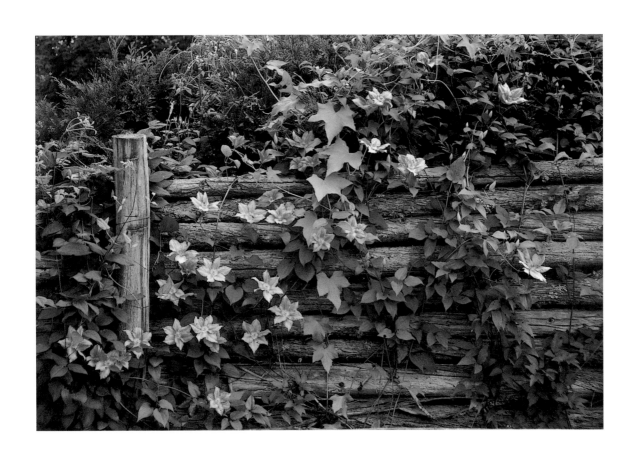

In the woods south of my house, the remnants of a cedar rail fence are strewn for more than half a mile (almost a kilometer) among the mosses and tall evergreens. Cedar is a beautiful wood that rots slowly; its fibers retain the history of a place for a very long time. These remnants bear testimony to the fact that over a century ago these woods were fields, that cattle may have grazed here, or simply that neighbors felt the need to demarcate the meeting of their properties.

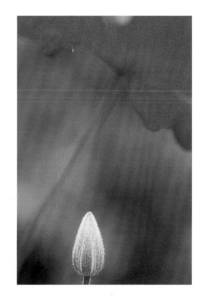

Many gardeners in these parts still build fences from both large and small cedar logs. The newer fences are usually short, but they still are functional, serving as supports for vines and backdrops for flower beds. Cedar fences appear naturally ornamental in a rustic sort of way. They "go with" vines and flowers, they fit quietly into the scheme of a garden, they add to the feeling of the place.

Cedar has another use: its green twigs make good tea. It's told that early sailors to North America made cedar tea to compensate for the lack of vitamin C in their diet, especially during the winter months. Pour boiling water over a few twigs, let them steep in the teapot for a few minutes, and the result is a light, slightly acidic drink that tastes pleasantly like cedar. Tea-drinking gardeners, take note!

Unlikely though it may appear, this garden bed filled with day lilies in bloom is the same bed shown on page 60. What a change eight weeks has brought! Now there's not a single red poppy to be seen.

We often lament the passing of the season for certain flowers, yet we also rejoice over the next flush of bloom. The same is true in our lives. We are thrilled when our children graduate from high school, and then some years later are thrilled all over again when they find love or a satisfying career. Our gardens — of every sort — are always changing.

These transitions can also be painful. I hate having to rip out the remains of what were recently magnificent plants, because I am reminded of what I have lost. And even though I realize that severe pruning will make my rose bushes a better shape and help them to bloom more abundantly next year, I loathe cutting back branches that only recently waved their colors in the wind. In fact, I cannot think of a more paradoxical activity than gardening — happiness and sadness balancing, the one fully dependent on the other.

At a profoundly fundamental level, however, the human spirit understands this paradox, accepts it, and rejoices in it. Deep down we know that, as much as we may yearn for flowers forever or eternal bliss, it really means eternal boredom. Changes, transitions, and developments bring meaning to our lives.

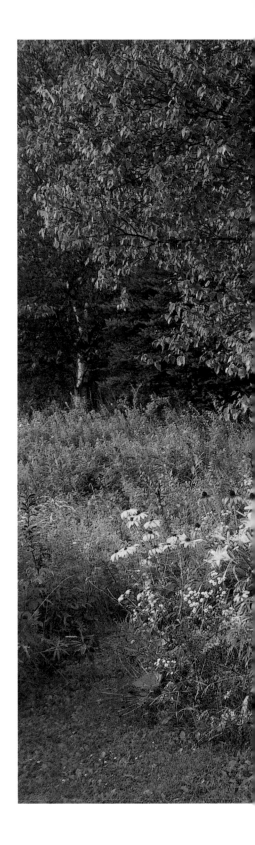

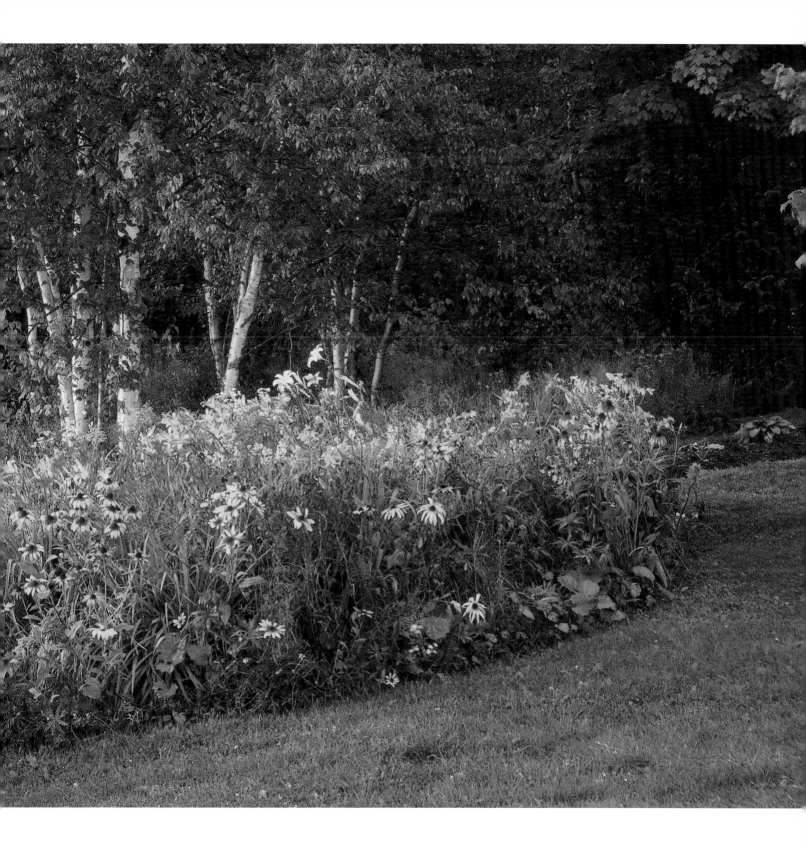

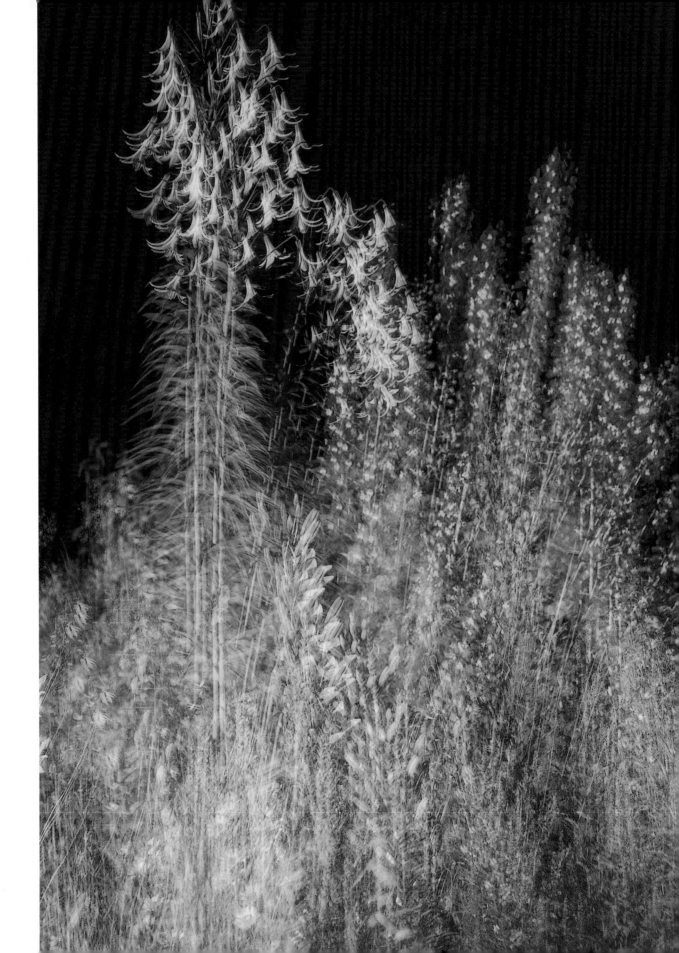

Every year at Shamper's Bluff there comes a time, usually early in July, when the vegetation becomes lush — taller and thicker and more abundant than I expected. Everything occupies more space than it's supposed to, including weeds!

This surfeit of beauty affects me in two quite different ways. My first reaction is like one I have earlier — every spring, in fact — that I can't possibly keep up with everything that seems to need doing, so I rush around in an unsuccessful attempt to accomplish the impossible. My second response, thankfully, is simply to let go. Let go and enjoy! Bliss out, it's summer!

Perhaps this photograph illustrates what I mean. The tall orange lilies were originally wild native plants that I moved to my garden from a wet field. I put them together with the purple delphiniums and other flowers that had come from a nursery or a packet of seeds, and nobody fought or even grumbled. They all just got on with growing and blooming, like they were supposed to. Very laid back behavior! Amazing, really! I couldn't help noticing that the plants and I were behaving very differently.

Whether or not the difference in our behavior was entirely in our genes, I can't say. However, there's nothing to prevent me from learning from plants. Some gardeners, of which I hope I'm one, note possible useful analogies between the way plants live and the way people live, and endeavor to put them into practice.

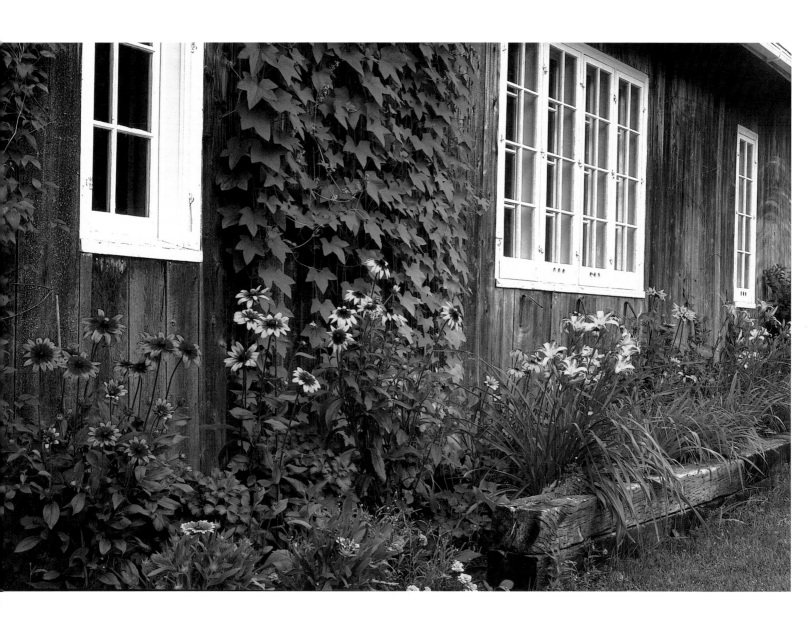

The cedar boards on the outside of my house came from big trees on my property that were dying, so I didn't feel bad about cutting them down. In time the trees would have fallen anyway, eventually rotting and becoming part of the soil again. But white cedar takes a very, very long time to decay and, besides, I considered that my use was also a legitimate one.

One spring I transplanted a few wild cucumber plants from the banks of the river, and set them along the back wall. They have been climbing the wall and self-seeding ever since. They make an attractive display of green leaves and, later, creamy white blossoms, as well as a pleasing backdrop for a narrow bed of domestic plants that I change a little every year, for one reason or another.

Like other garden beds here, this small house garden is a deliberate blending of the wild with the domestic, of natives with immigrants. I regard this mixing of species as a form of cultural activity, one that has relevance to many of our communities. Sometimes certain plants exhibit aggressive behavior, are reluctant to share resources, or are unwilling to get along with others. What used to surprise me, but doesn't any longer, is that frequently the various species settle their differences and get on with the business of living harmoniously. When one species steps too far out of line, either the community or I will take care of the problem.

If it weren't for fungi the planet would soon cease to function, probably within minutes. Like many other fungi, *Amanita* mushrooms (shown here) are important to the collective health of the forest, though I've also found and photographed them in open areas, where other species also live and do their work, often in gardens. For example, the delicious *Agaricus*, often called the "meadow mushroom," is common wherever there is decomposing manure of farm animals.

The abundance of mushrooms in this region at any given time depends to a large extent on weather conditions, but the climate encourages a huge number of species — with wild variations in color, shape, and size. Every few years I am overcome by "mushroom mania," a condition caused by the appearance of a bumper crop. For days I crawl around, peering at dead trees and stumps through a macro lens, though I enjoy photographing mushrooms in their overall habitat just as much as making close-up images.

The visible part of mushrooms, those weird constructions I love to photograph, are the reproductive organs. However, the daily work of most species is carried out by mycelia: fine, fibrous, root-like hairs that invade dead wood and other material, causing it to decay. Then bacteria take over and complete the process of making it part of the soil again. One day it occurred to me that we all garden with fungi and bacteria to a greater extent than we do with shrubs and herbs and grasses.

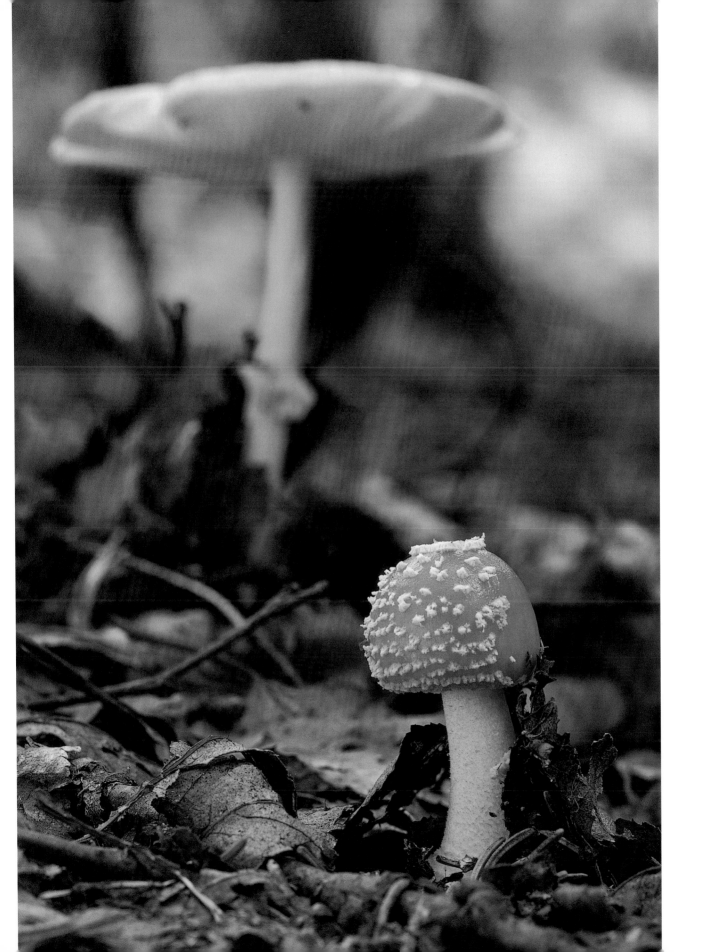

I grew up in an extended family and even as a child was accustomed to living with the young, the middle-aged, and the elderly. There was nothing strange about observing my relatives and neighbors growing older and more frail, watching them die, and then retaining their presence in memory. It all seemed so natural. It was just the way things were.

So this is a familiar scene to me and, in fact, to every hands-on gardener. The seed geminates, the plant grows, blossoms, is fertilized, sets seeds, and begins its return to the place of its birth. A necessary process on the one hand, but a divinely superfluous one on the other. Or so it seems to me.

Is the value of a life, any life, to be measured solely in biological terms? Or has it other worth? What of a human life? And what of a deer's life, or a daisy's? Is the meaning entirely inherent, genetically preordained? And what about the community life of an entire garden? Can we, as conscious human beings, find meaning in the life process, the whole cyclical process from beginning to ending to beginning?

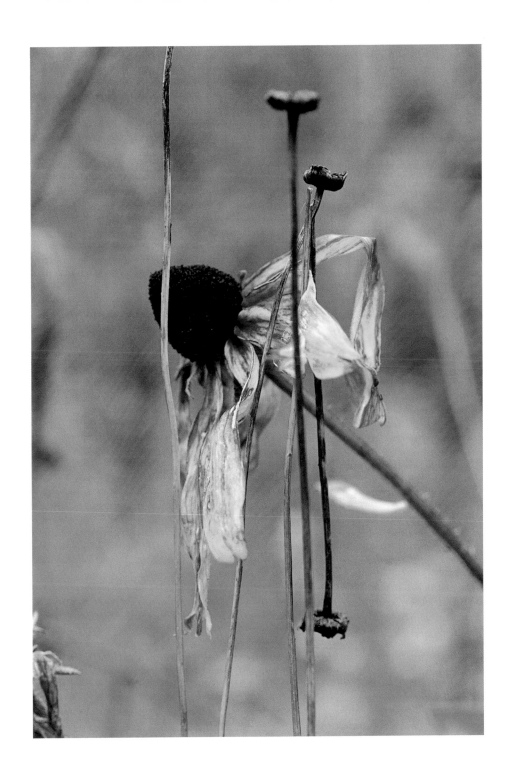

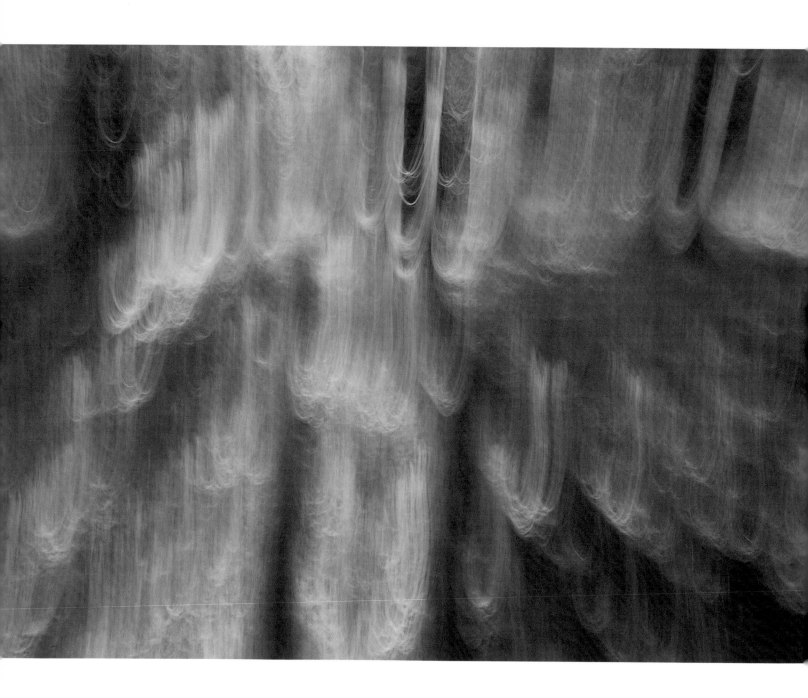

Recently I've been jumping up and down a lot — with my camera lens aimed at lupins, or liatris, or loosestrife, or, most of all, trees. Several times I've gone into the grove of cedar, spruce, and birch trees behind my house just when warm morning light spills through the branches and floods the forest floor and, while using a slow shutter speed, swung my camera up and down or on the oblique.

My visual interpretations of this favorite place, a small area from which I cleared away much of the dead undergrowth very shortly after I moved here, are consistent. In picture after picture the trees seem to be leaping, soaring, or dancing! While every photograph is unique, the overall visual impression is one of joy, ecstasy, and celebration.

If you believe that only a literal interpretation is real, or honest, or true, you'll probably think these don't look much like trees. And, you'll completely miss the real subject matter and the meaning of the image. I'm the subject matter, or more accurately, my mood is.

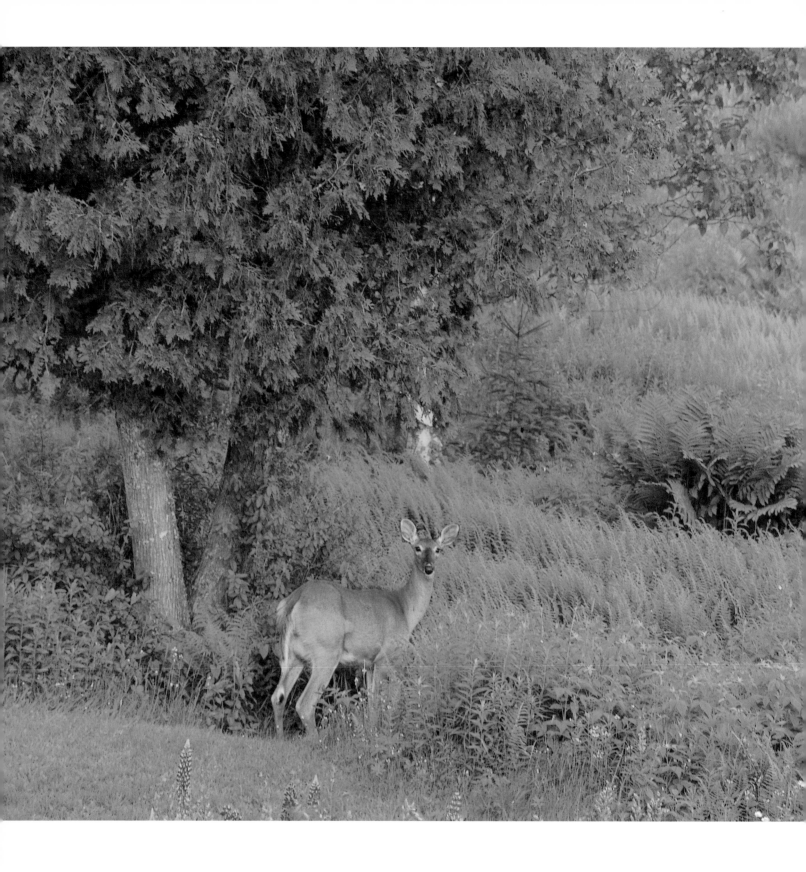

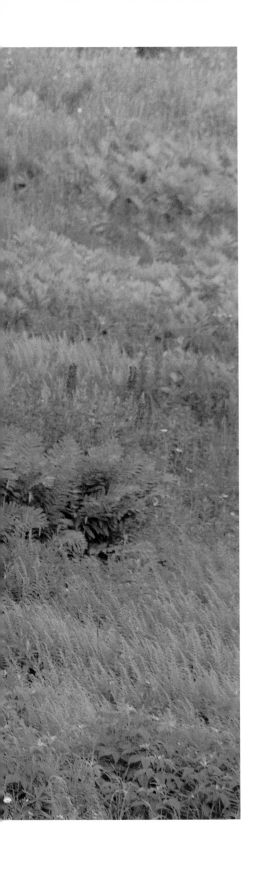

Deer are a problem for many North American gardeners. They love tulips, feast on hosta leaves, and also dine on tender branches of young ornamental fruit trees. In my garden, I've even seen a fawn with a rose clenched firmly between its teeth.

If you keep a dog, preferably a female who will have a defined territory, she will usually keep deer at a respectable distance; at least any dog I've had has done that. If you don't have a dog, you will undoubtedly try other potential remedies, almost all of which will fail. Some, however, do work well, when they are used carefully. For example, every spring I buy about a hundred bars of the original Irish Spring soap. I put one box by every hosta plant, just as the leaf stalks are beginning to emerge from the soil. The growing leaves soon obscure the soap, and the deer never touch them. If I wait until the deer have sampled a plant or two, I will lose the battle, as the deer learn that there are goodies beyond the distinctive odor.

To be honest, I'm as much a problem for the deer as they are for me. We share a mutual fondness for hostas — I enjoy their beauty, the deer enjoy their taste. It's one of those rare instances when no compromise between conflicting aesthetic and functional concerns seems possible.

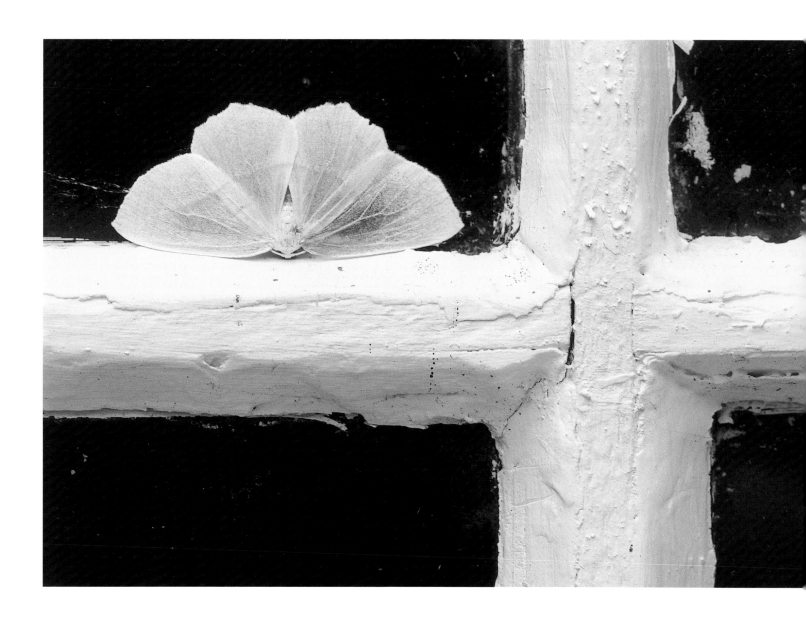

How does an insect know how to hide itself in full view of its prey? What puzzles me is not the fact of camouflage, but the making use of it. Who told this white moth to sit beside the white windowpane divider? And who or what told several gray moths to alight on the weathered cedar boards surrounding the window? It seems obvious to me that genes are involved, but that's about as far as I can get on my own.

If camouflage were a hundred percent effective, however, it would be a failure by nature's standards. If it functioned perfectly, the birds that eat these moths might starve. So some moths have to die for the good of the birds, but others have to live for the good of their own kind, which also serves the birds well in the future. Although we can accept this arrangement when it comes to moths and birds, we find it very difficult, if not impossible, to accept when nature treats human beings the same way: when a grizzly bear attacks a hiker, for example, or a mudslide sweeps away homes and people. Are humans special? Should humans be exempt from this law of nature, but not the other laws?

In fact, gardeners constantly sacrifice certain plants, "weeds," for example, for the good of other plants. This emotionally sustaining realm of beauty — the garden — also depends on our making use of natural laws, all of them.

AUTUMN

Season of mists and mellow fruitfulness

Close bosom-friend of the maturing sun;

Conspiring with him how to load and bless

With fruit the vines.

JOHN KEATS, "To Autumn"

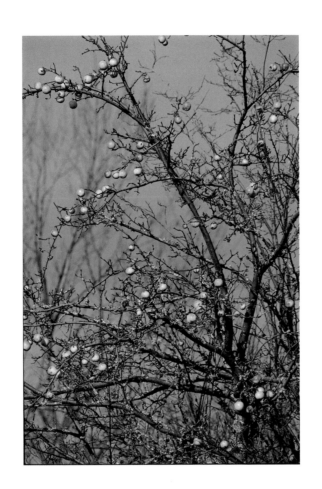

There are many evenings when I would like
the sun's long, slanting rays to continue shining down for a
few more hours. All the colors of blossoms seem especially
rich at this time of day, radiating an inner warmth. Inevitably,
however, Earth's rotation causes the magnificent display to fade
to a soft, dark haze that soon deepens to black. In that interim
between the setting of the sun and the coming of night,
clouds to the east that reflect the pink hues of the western sky
draw my eyes toward the heavens.

The colors of evening clouds are far more transient than
those of the flowers they illuminate, so I may go to a garden
bench or a deck chair where I can sit quietly and appreciate
fully the festival of light. Sometimes I make a few photographs,
but other times I will sit without my camera, because I don't
want anything to interfere with my experience of these holy
moments. Because nothing lasts forever, I make a daily effort to
savor "now."

And then comes the night, and if the air is warm enough
to make going for a jacket unnecessary, I may linger in the
hush. Here at Shamper's Bluff, it still is possible to listen to
silence.

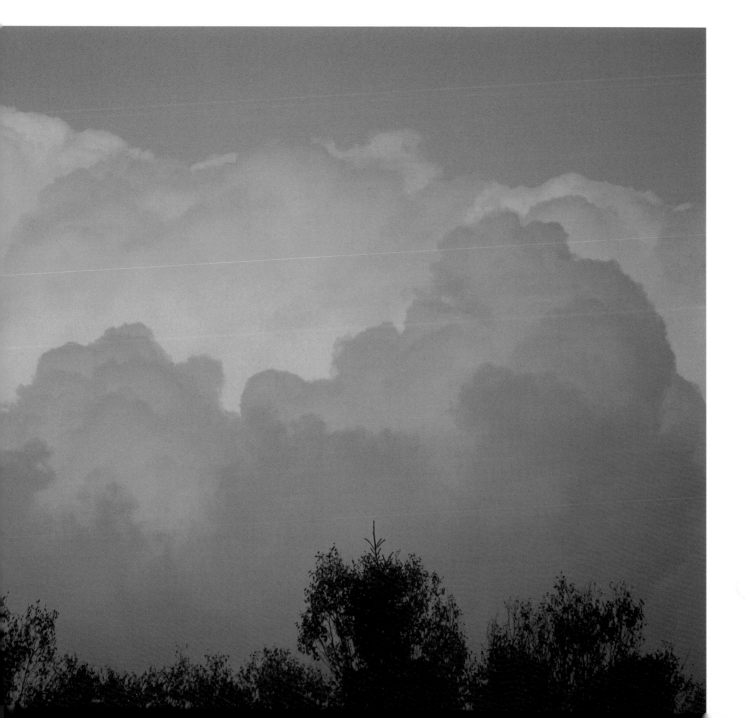

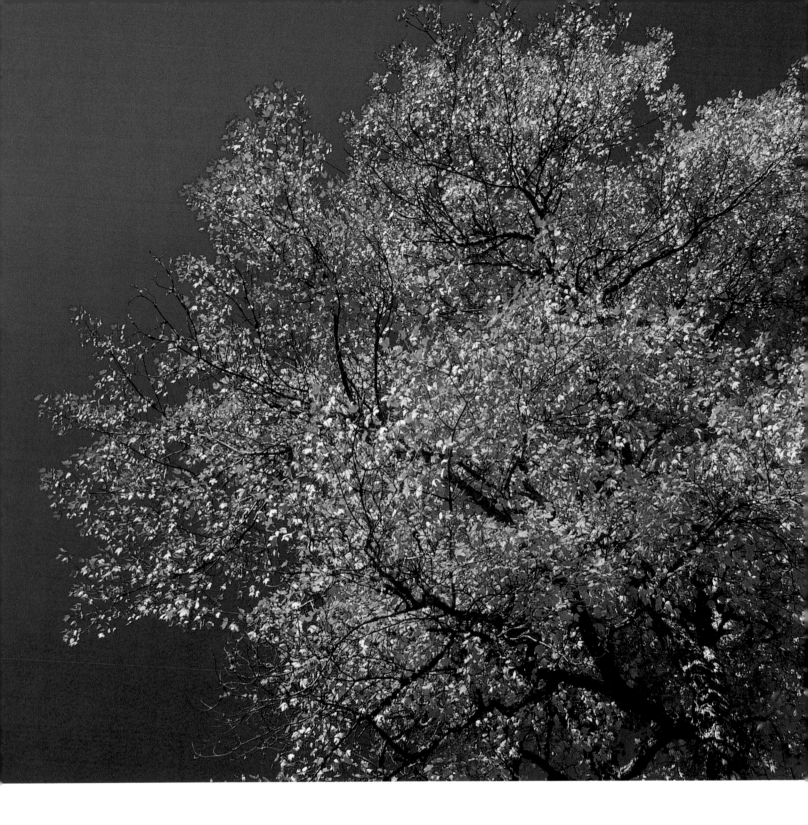

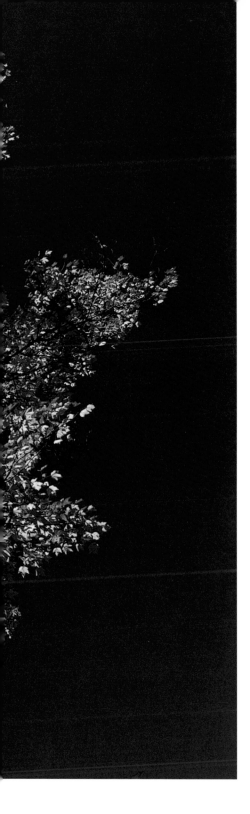

There was a long period, ten years perhaps, during which I photographed natural circles — circular rocks, clouds, flowers, and trees. Or, to be more accurate, the position from which I made the pictures caused the subject matter to appear circular, just like this maple tree one glorious autumn day.

I responded to the material at two levels — at the level of pure sensation, which was certainly the case here, and at a far deeper level, which is where the circles come in.

First, when I glanced upward, I remember feeling the sheer visual impact of the huge orange maple tree against the deep blue sky. I even remember shouting "Wow!" at the contrasting colors of the tree and the sky. That's all sensual stimulation and response.

Second, I decided to make a photograph, and there was a difference between what I was looking at and what I was actually seeing. The tree represented something whole, something complete for me. I didn't consciously think about that at the time; rather, I kept moving my tripod and camera position until the circle I knew to be possible appeared in my field of vision.

The circle has emerged in virtually every human culture as a symbol of perfection, and the impression that it gives of being self-contained expresses the idea of "the Self," that is, the inner self. We use circles both consciously and unconsciously to express our love of and desire for wholeness.

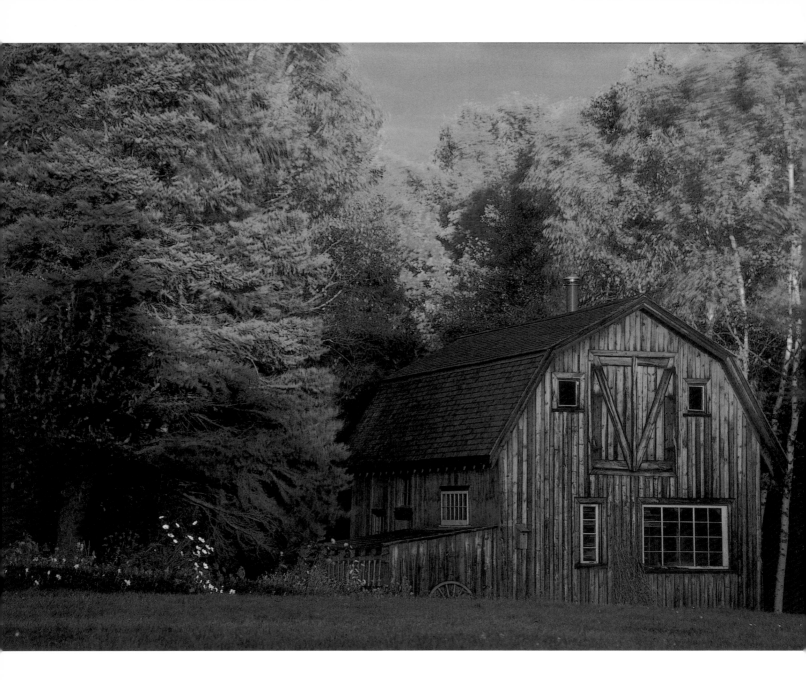

You can be certain that I didn't walk, but ran for my camera when the clouds parted and this intensely red sunset light flooded my barn and its surroundings. As I tore back into the field from my house, I was mentally composing the picture you see here. So, it wasn't difficult to find the spot I wanted. All of this was entirely instinctive — visual drama in nature gets me every time.

If I had had the time that evening, which I did not because the drama was all over within a couple of minutes, I would have moved in close to the late-blooming flowers and used the red barn or black shadows as a background for photographing them. Perhaps another time, though it could never be the same.

Moments like these are unexpected high points in the cycle of the seasons. Photographers and gardeners can't earn them, we certainly can't do anything to "deserve" them, but we can be grateful for their impact on our lives.

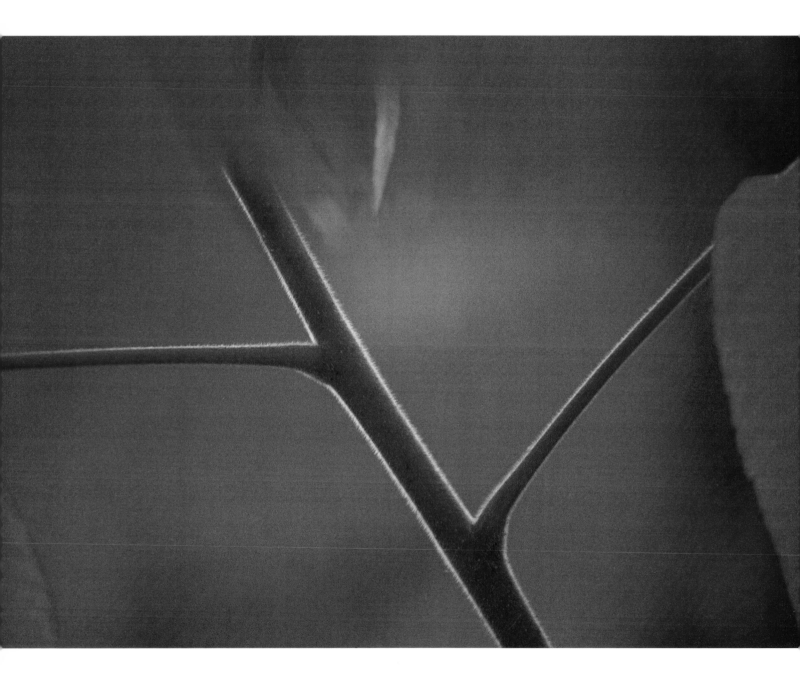

Aesthetic success always depends on knowing the craft well. Whether gardening, or painting, or making photographs — three media that require different tools and techniques — we are invariably working with visual design. It's the craft common to all three.

The designs we choose for our aesthetic endeavors often parallel designs in our lives. Take the lines and shapes in this picture of red sumach as an example. By turning the camera slightly, I've positioned the major line of the branch on the oblique. A slanting line always conveys a sense of the dynamic, of movement. I've also used this line to divide the picture space into two quite equal shapes, each of which is subdivided by the line of a leaf twig that reaches toward the edge. In these ways I've tried to convey a sense of vibrant life, coupled with a strong sense of balance — freedom and structure, dynamic and order working together — which is a personal goal.

Our garden designs, like designs we create in other visual media, may be either very consciously determined or spontaneous. The more spontaneous ones are usually the result of knowing the craft of design so well that we act or create unconsciously. We've already done the careful thinking, possibly over many years. But poor or ineffective designs — in gardens, pictures, or our lives — make clear that we have neglected to do our craft work.

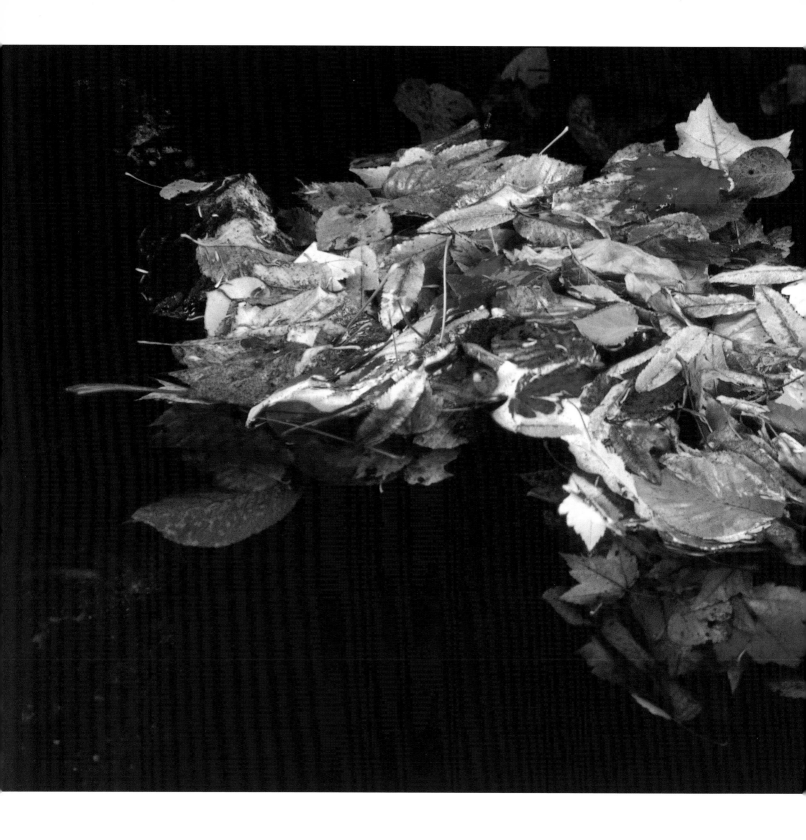

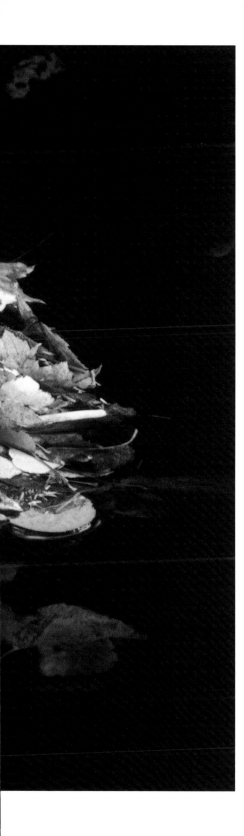

One of the nicest things about having a garden is the frequency with which we encounter unearned and undeserved beauty. These experiences that just seem to happen, that are given to us for no reason we can ascertain, I call "grace notes." Among the many definitions of grace, the one that holds the most meaning for me is "unmerited divine assistance" or, even better, "the quality of the divine breaking into one's life unexpectedly."

This little clump of colorful autumn leaves that formed in a pond seems far too insignificant to qualify for divine status, too ordinary for most people even to notice, yet it was an experience of grace for me. It's true that I arranged to have a stream altered slightly to create a pond, but that's all I did. I didn't plant the trees, I didn't arrange for the wind to blow the leaves off, and I didn't cause the movement in the water that brought the leaves here. The beauty just happened. For that, I am very grateful.

Frost tonight! Gardeners can feel it in the air. How we dread that inevitable prediction, especially when it comes while our gardens are still awash with color. We drag old bedsheets, blankets, and newspapers into the garden to tuck around plants that will not tolerate the freezing temperature. Everything in portable containers we move inside or, at Shamper's Bluff, into the woods, where the temperature will not dip quite so low. A few days, sometimes weeks later, we give up the battle and put the sheets away.

On clear mornings after that, we can see the rime even before the sun clears the horizon — patches of bare, brown soil now turned to gray, bright green leaves muted and misty, a strange pallor over the entire garden. The first morning we pull on a warm jacket and gloves and, because of our natural inclination to observe a disaster, trudge out of doors to inspect the damage. But the second and third frosty mornings lure us for a different reason — the radiant, sparkling beauty that awaits us among the daisies, the poppies, and the roses.

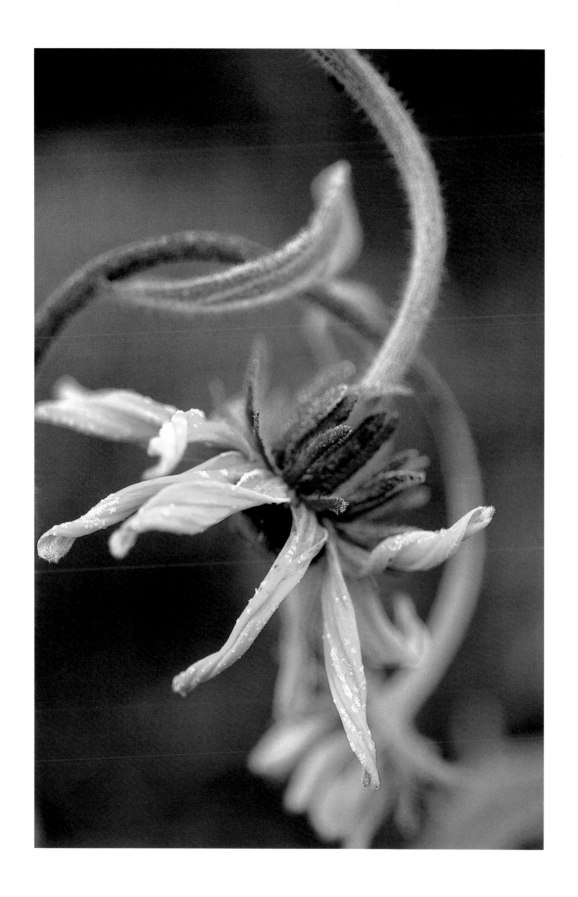

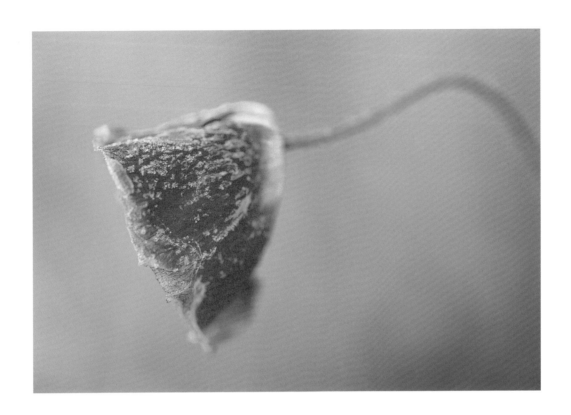

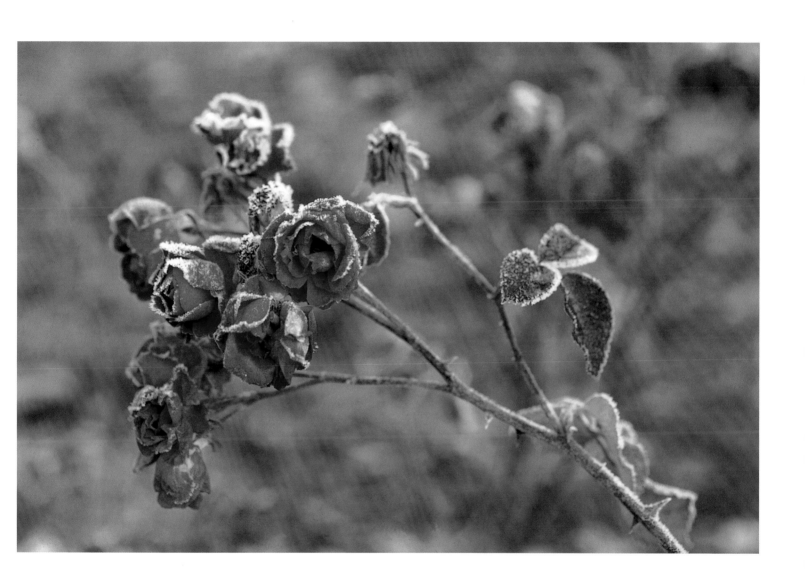

It doesn't happen often — snow falling when the leaves are in full autumn color — but when it does just about everybody grabs a camera and quickly "takes" a picture or two. Not content with this approach, I go out with my camera, a tripod, a couple of extra lenses, a pocketful of films, and lots of time. What's the hurry? This is a really important event, one that takes precedence over working at the computer, cleaning the house, or grocery shopping. Unlike some of these other calls on my time, snow falling on red maples can be a profoundly sensitizing, soul-making experience. To appreciate what's happening is to utilize nature for aesthetic and spiritual purposes, with no negative consumption of any sort.

Powerful identification with nature comes from giving nature time, and it often begins with an unusual occurrence — like snow on red maple leaves — that draws us away from daily routines. Anybody who enjoys natural things, who values the experience of walking in falling snow, canoeing in a morning mist, or picking raspberries in an old pasture wants time to savor the experience — to see and hear and taste and smell and, most of all, to feel.

The feeling is important. It's feeling that transforms us from observers into participants, that moves us to explore both outwardly and inwardly. Snow falling on red maples is a gift for the eyes, and it's also a balm for the soul.

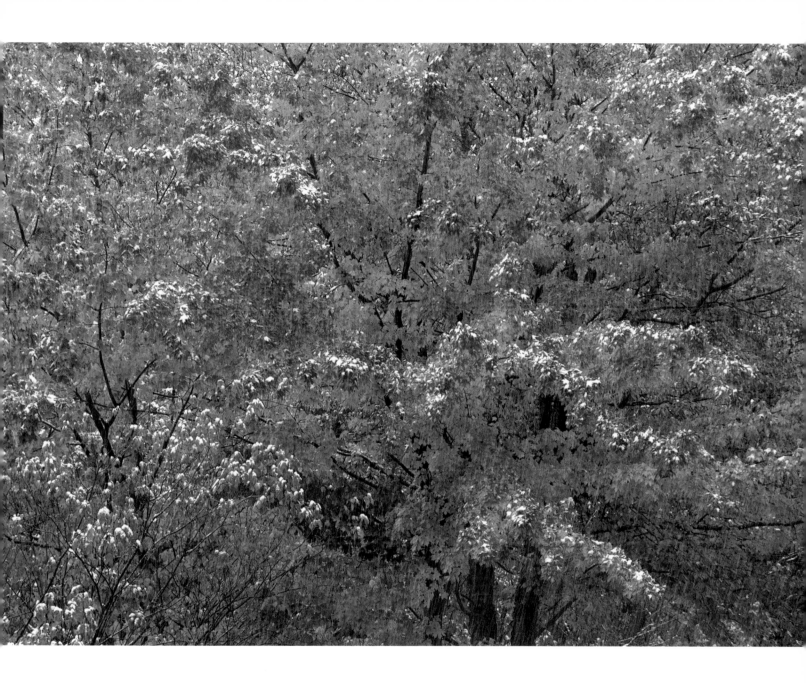

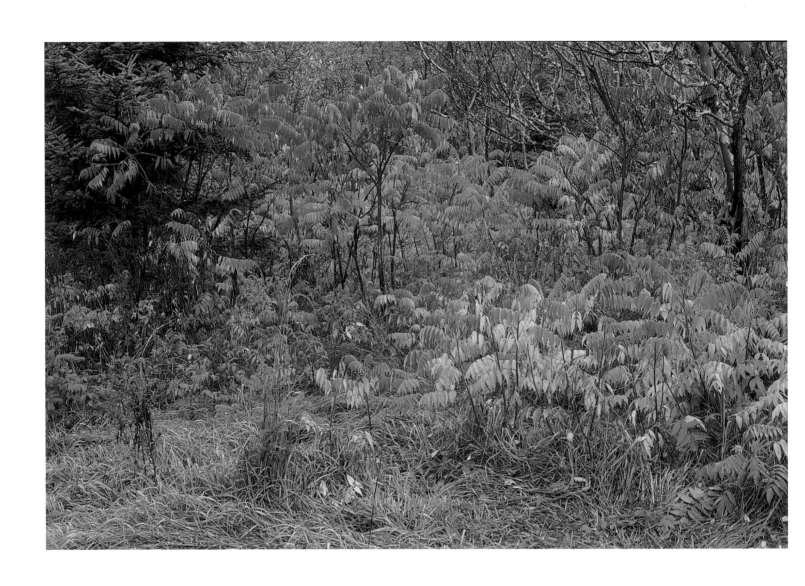

In autumn, sumach leaves change from green to an array of warm and brilliant hues, the many variations seeming to depend on soil, moisture, and exposure. For years I have enjoyed the year-round beauty of sumach bushes growing in the wild, and also in areas near my house where I have planted them among hay-scented ferns.

When I first discovered this colorful group growing in the nearby woods, I drove the short distance to my parents' home and told my mother I had a surprise for her, "Something I know you'll love seeing." My mother was in her late eighties and quite frail, so when we arrived at the edge of the woods, I told her that I would pretend to be a horse drawing a cart, and she would be the cart. I stuck my hands out behind me, she grasped both of them, and I slowly pulled her through the bushes and trees to the spot where the sumachs stood. As soon as she saw them, she let out a little gasp, and the two of us stood side by side, gazing silently at the autumn colors set among the greens.

After about fifteen minutes my mother said, "Thank you for bringing me here." With that I stuck my hands out behind me again, and we left the woods.

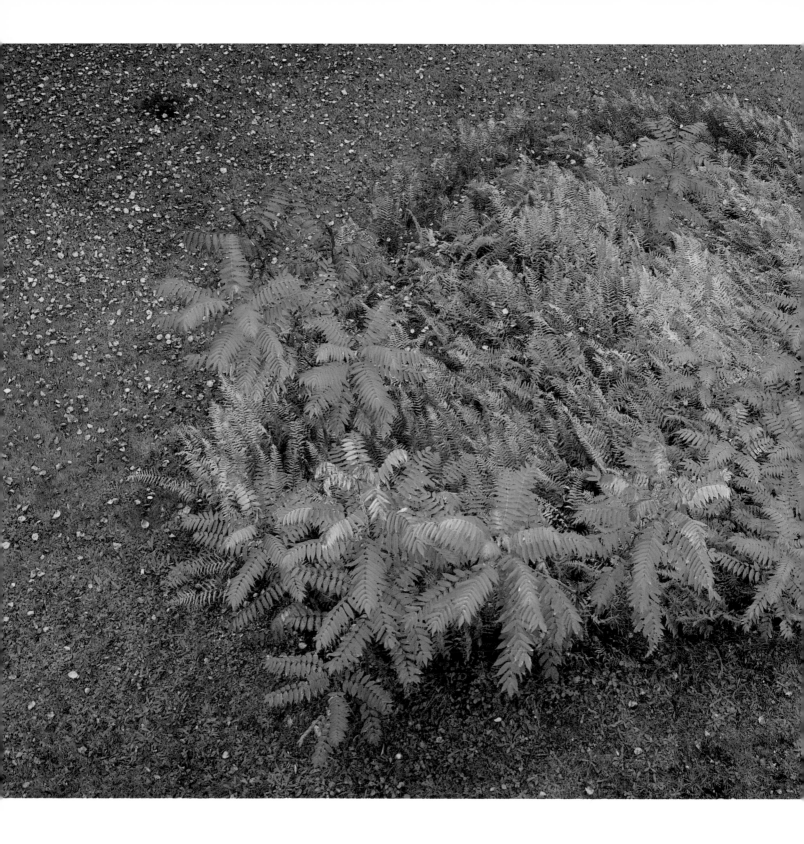

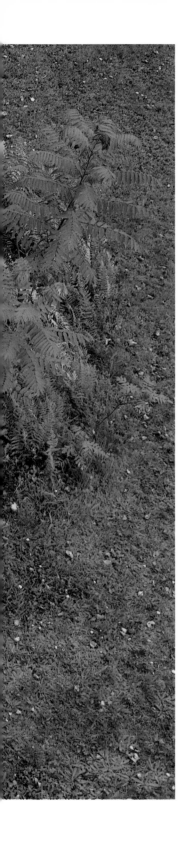

I am very fond of gardening with plants that are indigenous to Shamper's Bluff. They grow well if I transplant them to a habitat similar to their wild one or to one created for them. They cost me nothing, except the time and energy to move them, and they probably won't require any fertilizers. More importantly, the leaves and flowers of many native species are very beautiful. I like having them close by where I can easily enjoy them, year-round in many instances.

In this bed I've brought two native species together: hay-scented ferns and sumach shrubs. This photograph was made in early October. Compare it with the photograph on pages 148–149 which is the same bed from exactly the same point of view, but made in late November of another year, and with my German shepherd, Tosca, who decided to pose for the picture, something she did rather regularly.

Hay-scented ferns and sumachs combine well both horticulturally and visually. The sumachs need pruning occasionally to keep them from becoming too tall and leggy. The ferns are utterly care free. You can't have easier gardening than that!

Many years ago a previous owner clear-cut this area behind my house, and when the forest grew back, all the trees were more or less the same age. The competition was fierce, and the struggle about equal. By the time I arrived, the woods were virtually impenetrable, with thousands of dead trees crowded together, unable to fall and rot. The forest floor was also lifeless. So, with the help of a couple of friends, I began a process of selective cutting, felling most of the dead trees and a few living evergreens that would otherwise dominate the natural regrowth of native species. Then we piled the debris and, during the winter, burned most of it, leaving a few piles for birds and animals to use for protection.

It took only one year for the forest floor to change radically. A host of flowering woodland plants moved in, and by the second spring were blooming abundantly — goldthread, star flowers, and bunchberries, to name a few. Various ferns that had barely survived in the crowded darkness quickly expanded their range and tripled their size. Birds I had not heard for a long time began calling and singing in the trees. Deer and other mammals moved back, and even an occasional bear and moose passed through. I marked out a few walking trails, and from one of them I made this picture.

These woods have changed since then, because a forest is a dynamic, creative community. Whether it's forests or fields, there's no better way to garden than simply to help the community do what comes naturally.

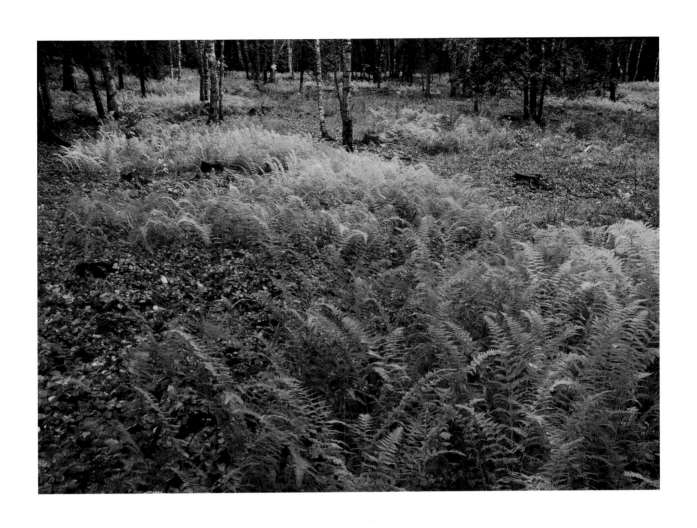

The view from my house is always

magnificent, but never more lovely than late on a sunny autumn afternoon when mist hangs over the river. It gives me deep satisfaction to know that this land will never be "developed," a euphemism for destroying the fabric and appearance of natural communities.

Some people say that our country is underpopulated, as if humans were the only species living here. But the best possible use of land is to leave it alone — let the trees and other plants filter the air, and allow the soil to keep the water clean. Only then can all the elements and species work together to maintain global temperatures that will prevent us from frying or, alternatively, freezing to death.

Equally important are the aesthetic and spiritual sides. Useful though they may be, parking lots provide neither biological nor spiritual enrichment to our lives. Strip developments have no value in nature's scheme of things, but wild places are of primary importance. Many modern constructions — casinos, luxury resorts, superhighways — exist only by sacrificing places like the one in this photograph. What will happen to our sense of awe and wonder when air and light pollution extinguish our view of the stars? What will life be like without a garden?

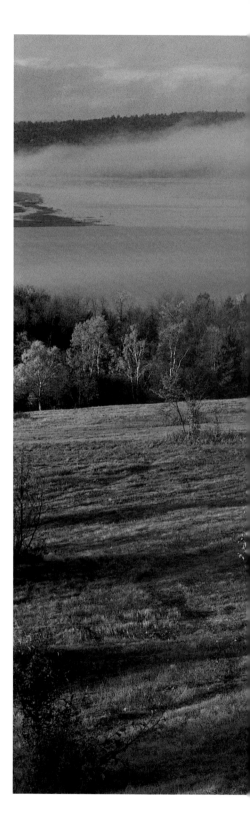

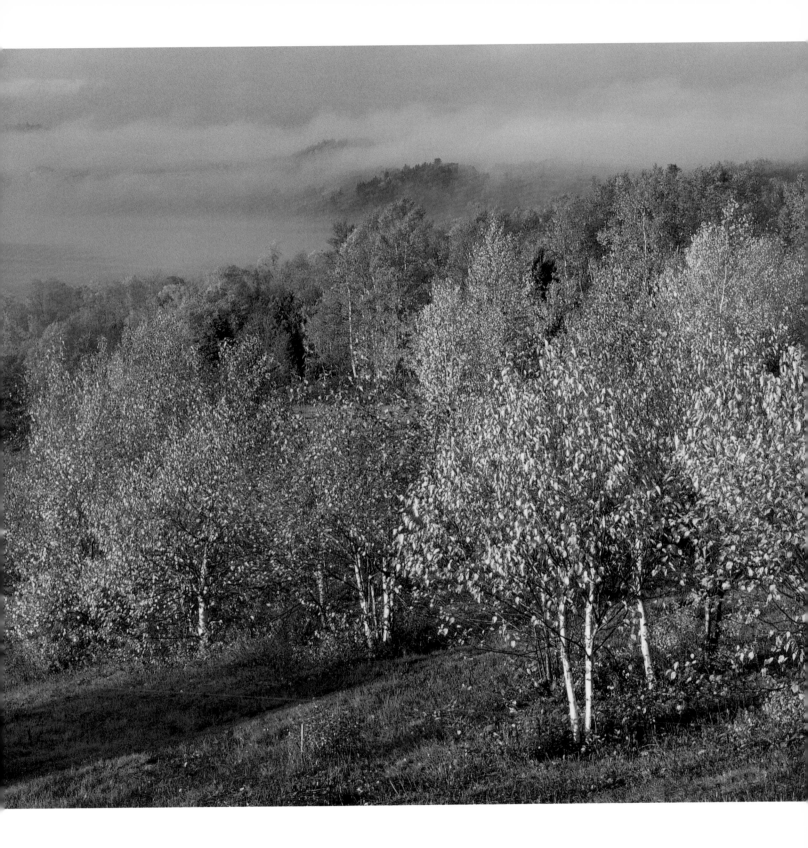

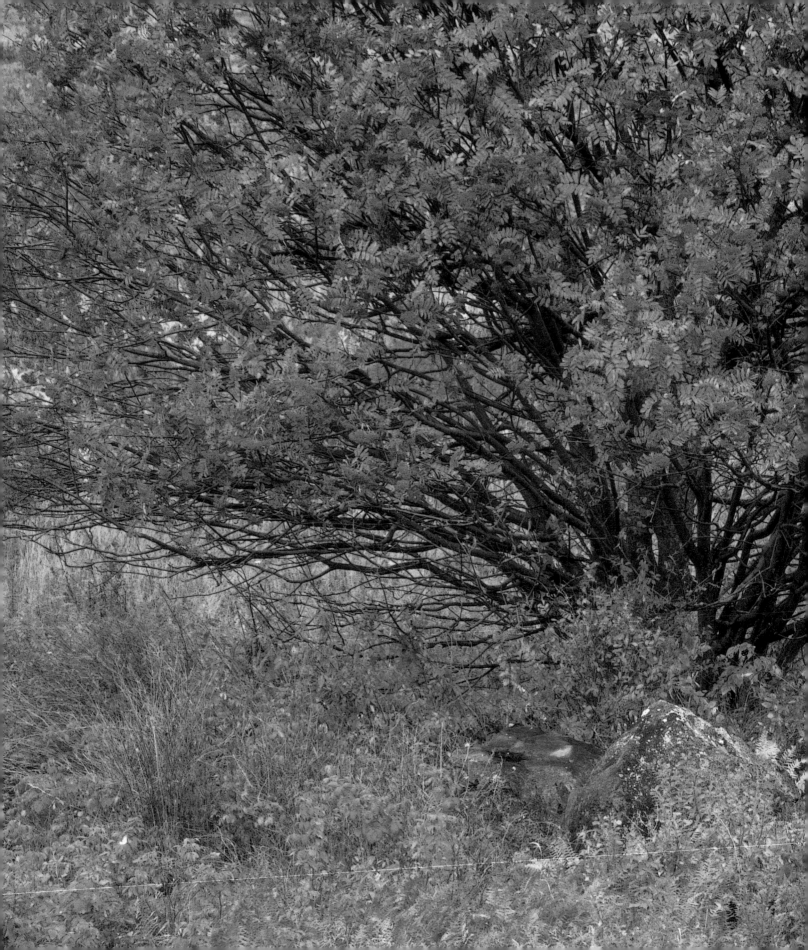

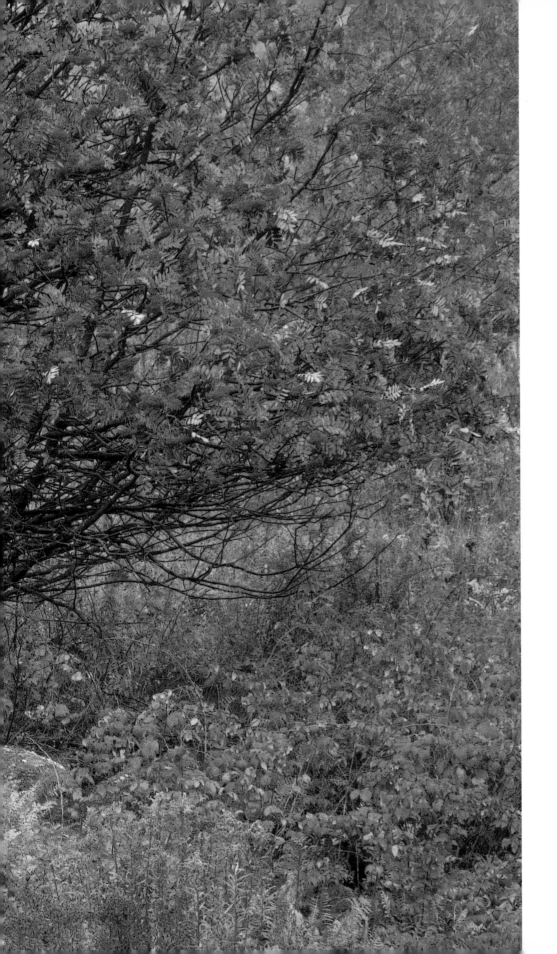

As different as they may appear, these golden birches are the same ones in the photograph on page 135. The two photographs represent two very different ways of looking at exactly the same thing.

The first night I was so taken with the warm, slanting light illuminating the trees that I chose to make a documentary image. The second night, passing by at sunset, I felt the leaves shimmering in the breeze, and watched the trees themselves swaying back and forth. They were alive! Dancing! Could I document this well? Probably not, but I could certainly create an impression to convey the feeling.

From time to time I invite other photographers to make pictures in my garden, and I've noticed over the years that the more ecstatically or fully they respond to the myriad blends of tones and colors, the more likely they are to make impressionistic renderings, rather than visually accurate descriptions. I do wonder occasionally about the relationship between expression and inner freedom. Would a really rigid person fling brilliant colors at a canvas? Or dance the limbo? Or ever make a revealing impressionistic painting or photograph?

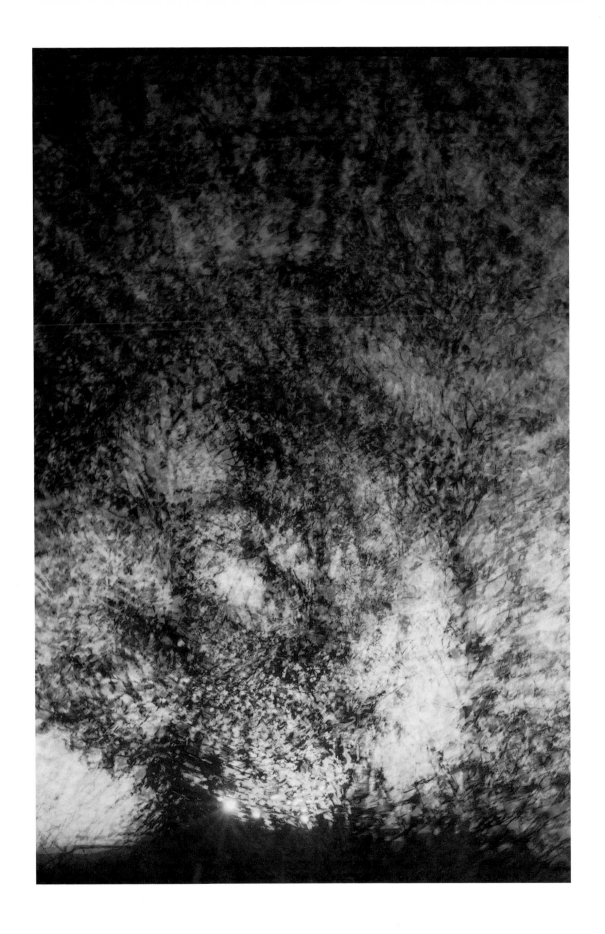

Dying hosta leaves always remind me of my mother in the final days of her life. It may be the beauty of their pallid hues — white, creamy beiges, grays, and hints of blue. It may be their weakness. It may be the leaf stalks reaching out like arms, the leaves resting like hands, waiting to be picked up and held. Or it may be because my mother died late in the year, when the hosta leaves were dying too. My memory of my mother stretches back to when she was quite young, and I see the progressive aging of hosta leaves as a metaphor of my mother's changing countenance.

This red maple leaf seems like a Remembrance Day poppy, though I did not place it there. Perhaps I left it there for what it symbolizes. I'm never sure about things like that. I do know that each year, when my stunning hostas complete their vibrant lives in what seems like serene and quiet death, I feel a pervading sadness. It is finished, and there is nothing more I can say or do.

And yet the hostas come back to life in the spring, and my mother too lives on. It is because of her that I have a garden.

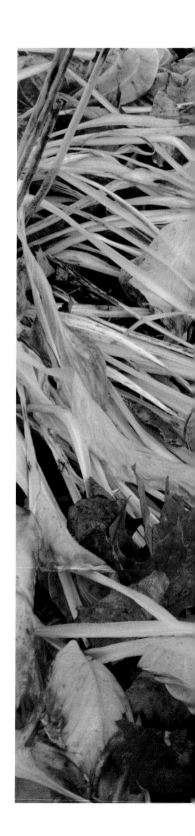

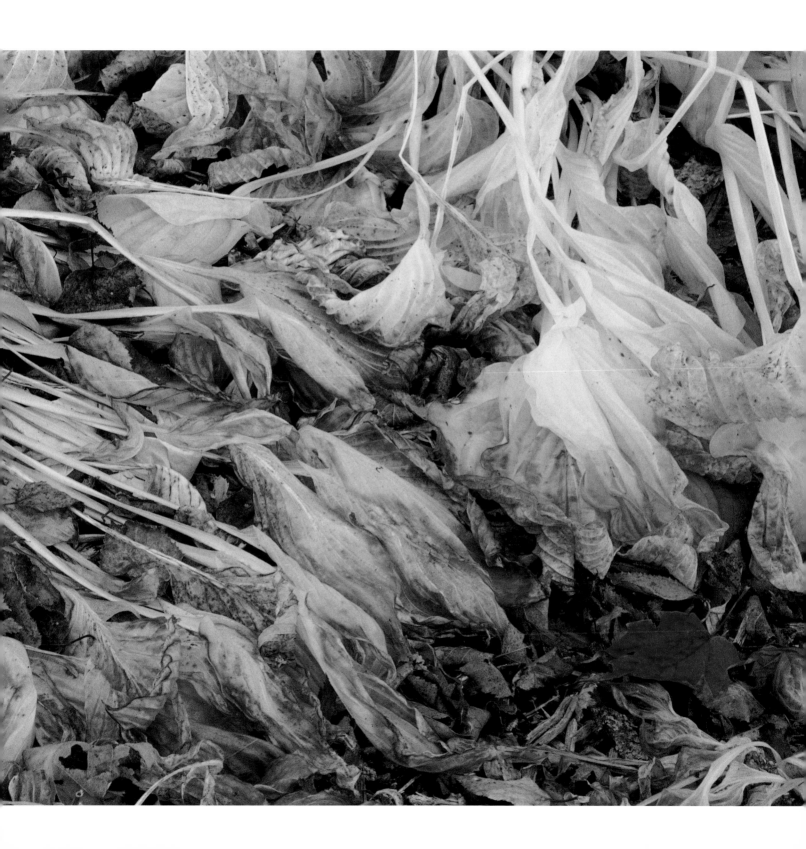

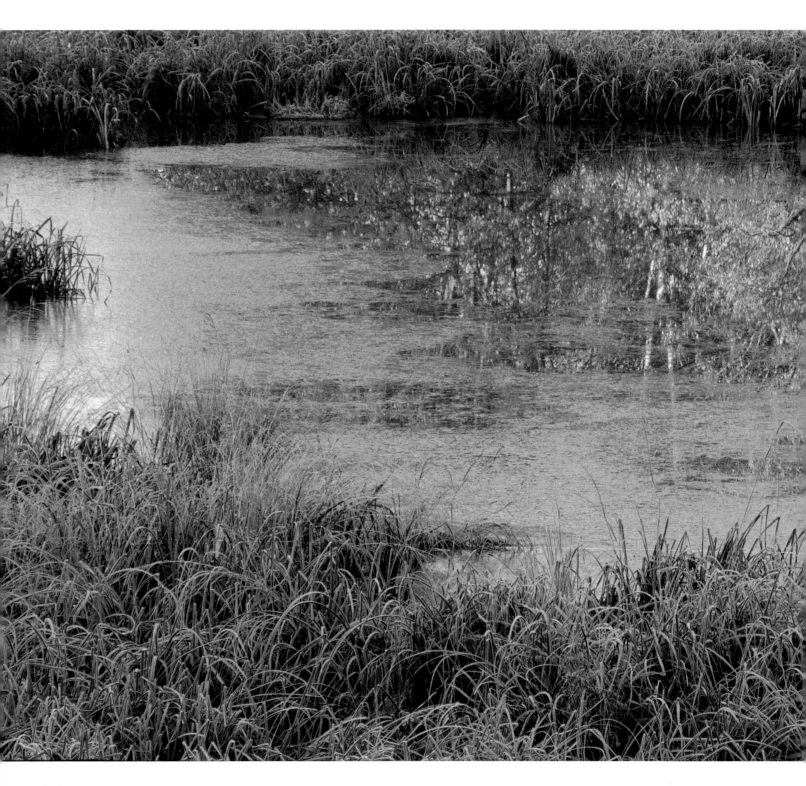

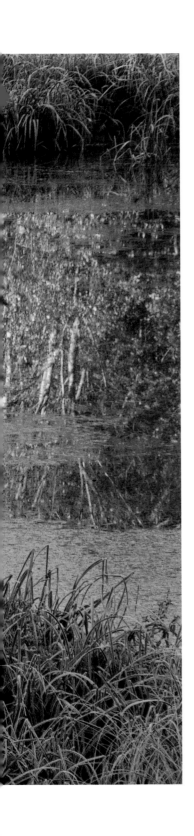

Although we regret the fleeting nature of many things in our lives, their physical passing does not mean that they have been lost. The special moments that we experience in gardens and in wild places live on in our memory, and in our pictures. Like favorite aunts and uncles, they enrich and influence the progress of our lives, and in that important sense have an enduring legacy.

The opportunity to enjoy a few moments like this on a frosty autumn morning is more than enough reason to incorporate a pond, a natural pool, or a small body of water into a garden area. The water will also provide reflections of other colors over the course of the year, and perhaps some quite beautiful ice patterns during the winter months, as in the photograph on page 173.

We can often choose what we remember, and the best way to do that is to appreciate it at the time. If we walk quickly by colorful reflections, they will surely not be part of our future. If we pause to observe their colors and patterns closely, however, we will not only make them into positive memories, but also increase our sensitivity to other such moments of beauty. In both these ways we are giving a gift to ourselves.

November is an in-between month in the garden. The brilliant reds, oranges, and yellows of autumn shrubs have softened to gentle hues or disappeared altogether, but the strong, contrasting whites and blacks of winter have yet to appear. It is a time of subtlety, restraint, and delicacy.

Because I mow only small patches of fields near my house and have many paths through wild and semi-wild areas, grasses take on a visual importance in late autumn that is greater than at any other time of year, their thin silver and brown lines cross-hatching and weaving intricate tapestries of incredible variation. Similarly, low shrubs, such as the cranberries, wild roses, and wild cherries that dominate this mix of bushes, sometimes have an aura unlike anything seen at the height of autumn. If we have learned to hate November, however, the way we have been encouraged to loathe dandelions, we may fail to recognize its subtle beauty.

I am deeply attracted by secondary hues — browns, beiges, off-purples, gray blues, creams — and by very desaturated primaries. These in-between colors give to late autumn a quiet mood unlike that of any other time of year, except for those few days before the first greens of spring emerge.

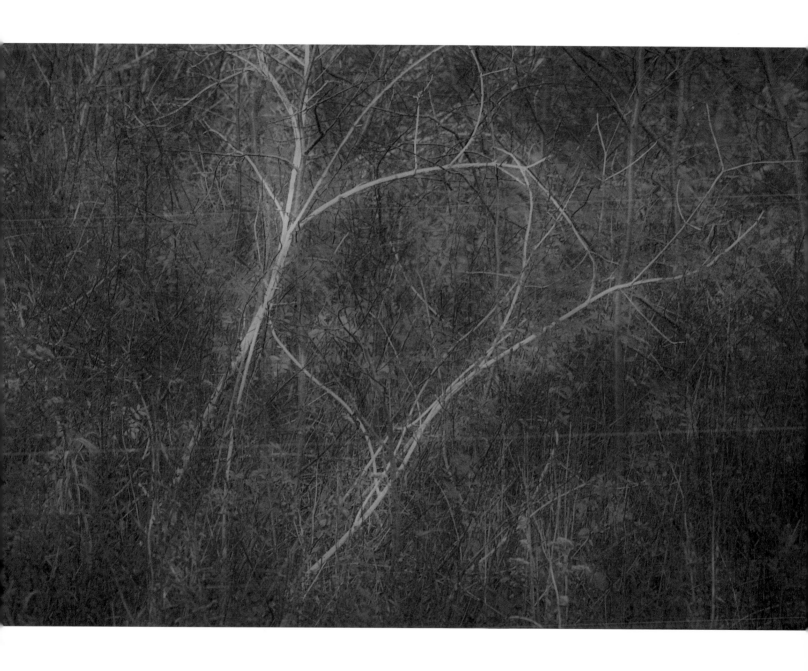

One late autumn afternoon, as my sister and I were walking along a woodland trail, we paused to sit on some old mossy stumps. As we sat there chatting, both of us gradually became more and more aware of our immediate surroundings, and frequently commented on natural objects or details that attracted our attention. That afternoon, the longer we sat and talked, the more my eyes were drawn to the interweaving of tree trunks, branches, and barren twigs. During the many years that I've been making photographs of natural things and situations, I've gradually reduced my concentration on close-up details of natural objects and developed a very strong interest in habitats, communities, and relationships, both biological and visual ones. This impressionistic image of the trees I was observing that afternoon is an expression of that development.

The difference in response that people sometimes have between looking at a photograph of a rug I own and looking at this photograph is interesting. I wonder if one viewer's dismissive response of this picture indicated a hesitancy to admit he didn't know "what" the subject matter was, but felt he should. Or, was he saying, "What good is this? It doesn't tell me anything." Why is a pattern that's acceptable in a rug, a painting, or even a forest not acceptable in a photograph?

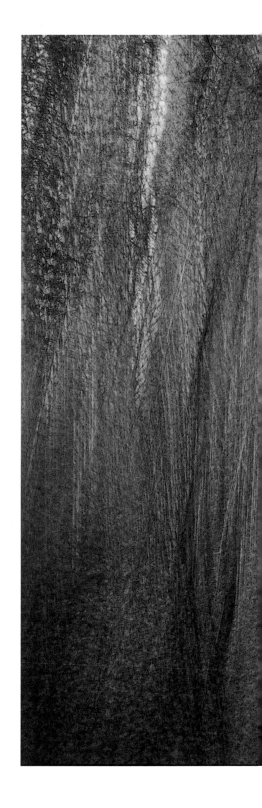

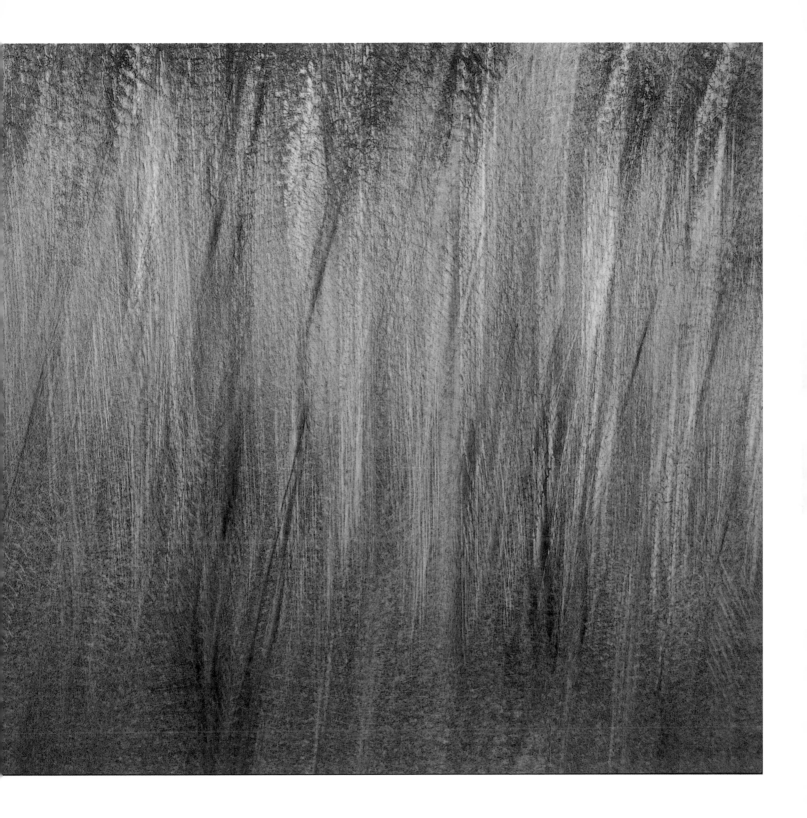

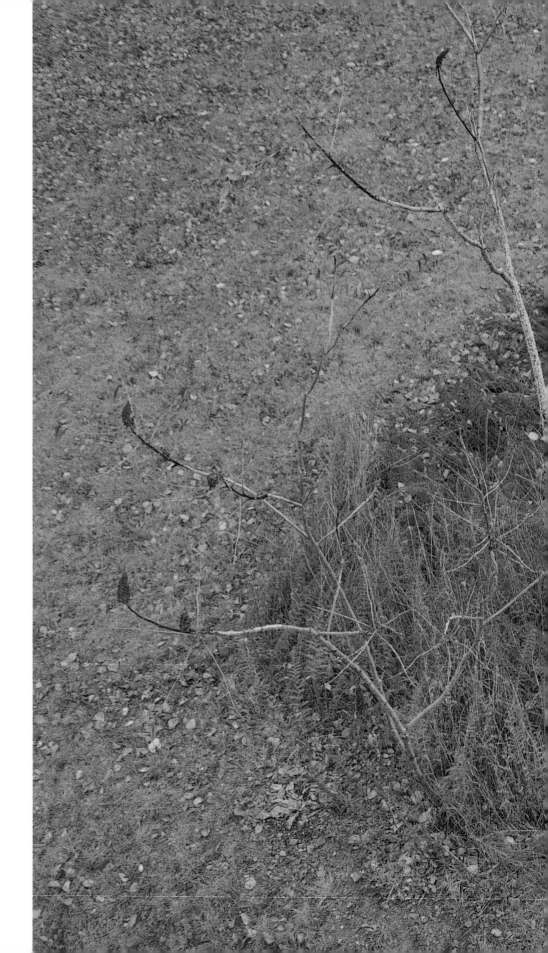

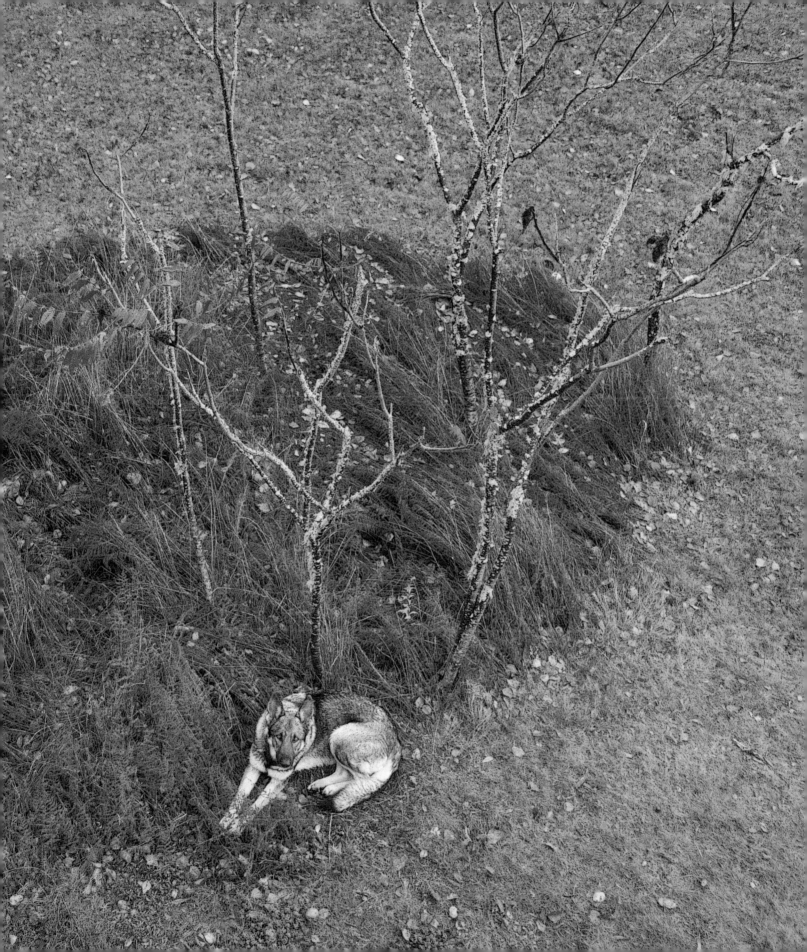

When I die this path will soon disappear. It's a perfect symbol for the fact that, except for very, very few people, each of us will be remembered for only a short time, usually no longer than the last living person who knew us.

There are times when a thought like this tends to get us down, to depress us. But, let's consider the alternative. While everybody dreams at one time or other of living forever, the greater challenge is living in the present. What's the value of living a couple of billion years if we spend it dreaming about the next two billion? What's the point of living at all if we constantly postpone the experience, if we never catch up with the future?

Some days the present, my present, is in walking this path. Its very existence testifies to my being there. The ferns, trees, birds, and other inhabitants of the old pasture are my companions, but only if I engage them with my eyes, my ears, and my other senses. When I recognize and value their existence, they enrich my life aesthetically and spiritually, though in many ways they would still contribute to my life even if I were utterly unaware of them.

Not all gardeners enjoy wild places or paths as much as I do, but all of us, at heart, are sensuous people. The more we engage our senses, the more we live in the here and now, then the greater our experience of wonder and joy will be.

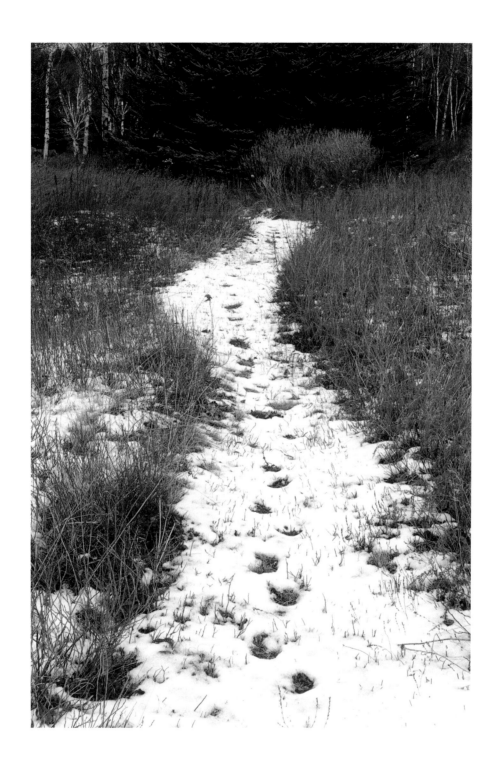

WINTER

The snow came last night. She left before the dawn, bestowing in her wake a benediction upon the earth. Now, in morning light, she greets us gently, a prayer shawl donned upon the land.

KENT NERBURN, "A Haunting Reverence"

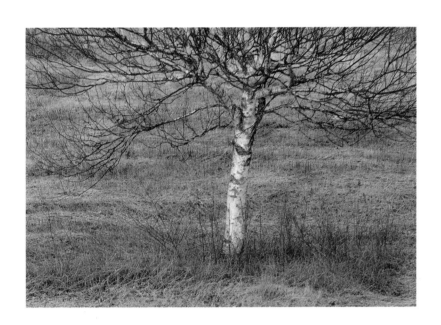

The first snowstorm is always the best. If the flakes fall thick and big and fluffy and the wind is not strong, there is an hour or two of magical transformation. Sometimes the snow melts and there's a first snow all over again. Some years at Shamper's Bluff that happens several times.

My favorite place to be at times like this is in the woods near my house. The snowflakes drift down through the open spaces between the trees, slowly covering the swathes of brown leaves and needles that carpet the forest floor, but somehow delineating and emphasizing the lines of exposed roots. I await this annual natural etching process, usually between the end of November and the middle of December, with considerable anticipation, realizing all the while that it may mark the passing of autumn and the beginning of a season that is always cold and snowy, and seems to last about six weeks too long.

The fall of the snowflakes is interrupted by the branches of evergreen trees, so under the spruce, fir, hemlock, and cedar, large brown circles begin to appear as the snow slowly fills in the open places. There is something primal about these remarkable patterns. I feel I am in the presence of ancient things.

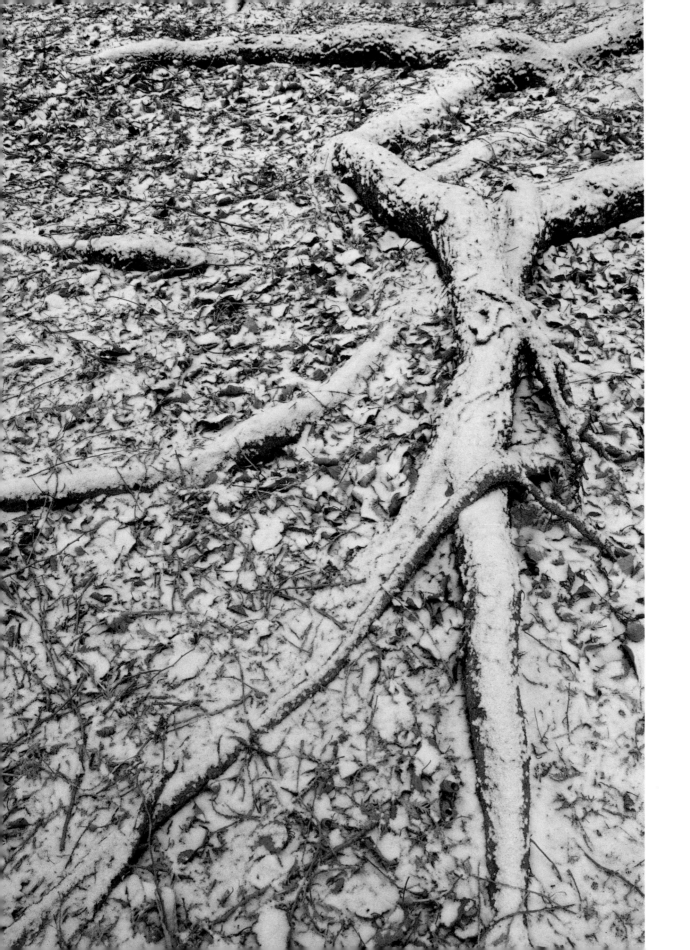

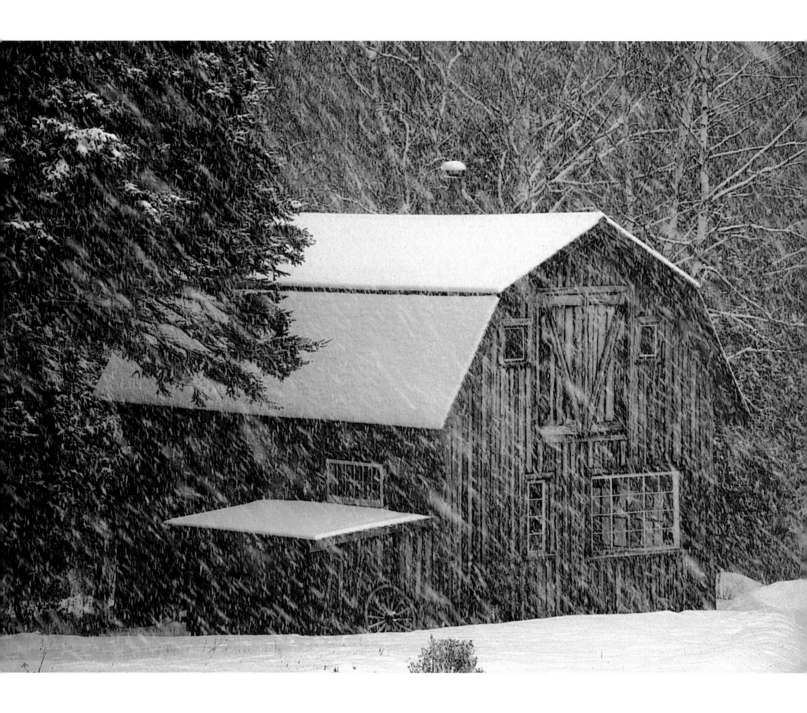

When I was a young boy, the seed catalog

from Dominion Seed House arrived in January. No matter how deep the snow or intense the cold, I was immediately into gardening — in my imagination. I would retreat to the comfort and solitude of a haymow and there, hidden from the family's view, I would indulge my dreams.

Despite the fact that my father kept several hives of bees and sold honey, he always admonished that flowers were "completely useless," and from time to time went on an eradication campaign by running over them with farm machinery or turning pigs lose to grub them out. Even at a relatively early age, I knew in my heart that "usefulness" was not the be-all and end-all of existence. I was extremely diligent in protecting my little plot of ground and grasped every opportunity to show off my flowers to every aunt, uncle, and visitor who dropped by. Their lavish praise became my best defense. Thus, I was able to accomplish in the summer what I had dreamed about in the middle of winter. Since those days I've come to realize that everybody has a "dream catalog" and everybody needs to find a haymow for browsing through it. That's where serious gardening always begins.

Every garden needs a bush, or two, that produces some sort of colorful fruit or berry. If the berries hang on into the winter, they add brightness and cheer to a garden and possibly provide good food for birds when they need it. These high-bush cranberries along my driveway do both of these things, and one morning after a fresh snow their beauty rivaled anything I'd enjoyed during the summer.

One of my neighbors competes with the birds for high-bush cranberries. She makes a delectable, tart jelly from them. Fortunately, high-bush cranberries are fairly numerous around here, so the birds have plenty for winter dining, my friend picks all she wants for her jelly, and there are still enough left for me to photograph on snowy days.

Besides high-bush cranberries, I have near my house a mountain ash that produces large clusters of reddish orange fruit (see pages 136–137), which evening grosbeaks and crows consume voraciously in the autumn. The tree is usually picked clean in one day. A large hawthorn nearby is the next target, but for some reason the birds never take the fruit from a hawthorn bush that grows near my front door, so I am able to photograph it right through the winter.

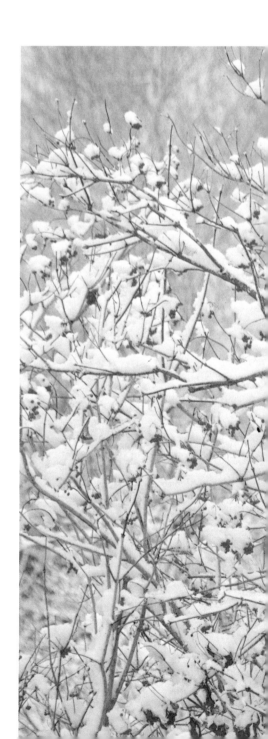

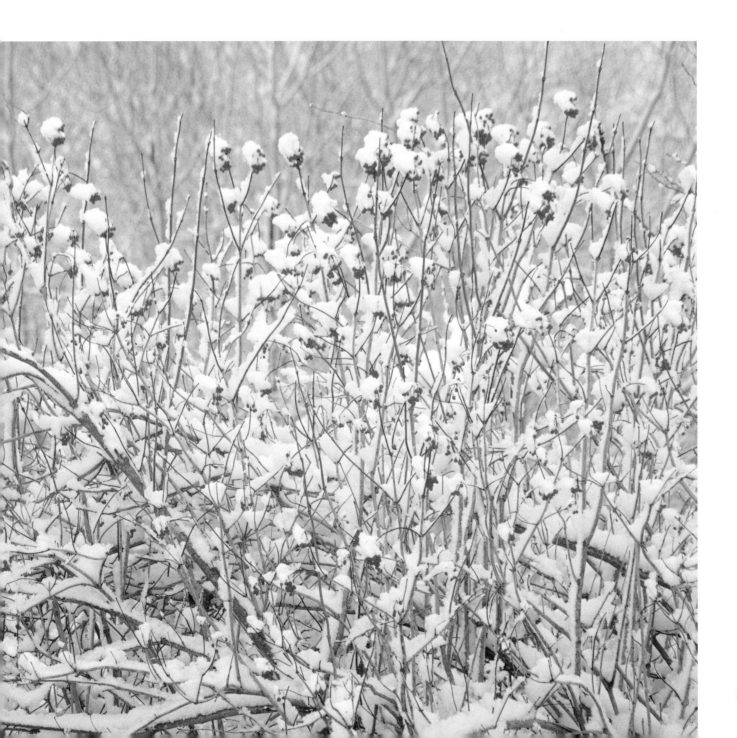

Late one overcast winter day, a sudden burst

of sunlight instantly diverted my attention away from my computer to the view through the nearest window. I had a camera on a tripod nearby, and I quickly moved it to the window and began photographing through the glass. This is one of several images I made in the few minutes before the break in the clouds closed up.

The sight of sparkling, ice-covered trees returned me to my childhood, to days when I tromped through old pastures and wandered down forest trails overhung with shimmering branches. I long for those days again, but of course I can never quite recapture them. Good memories are always bittersweet.

The magical trees outside my window also reminded me of childhood Christmas trees, which always seemed so wonderfully tall and grand. My mother knew how to hang those old lead icicles through the branches so they looked mysterious and magical. In those days, before electricity came to the farm, the light from a kerosene lamp would flash spectral highlights from the very center of the tree, as if falling stars had become snagged in the branches.

Caught between then and now, I stood at the window long after the sunlight had faded, a mute witness to the old, innocent days that will forever give meaning to my present.

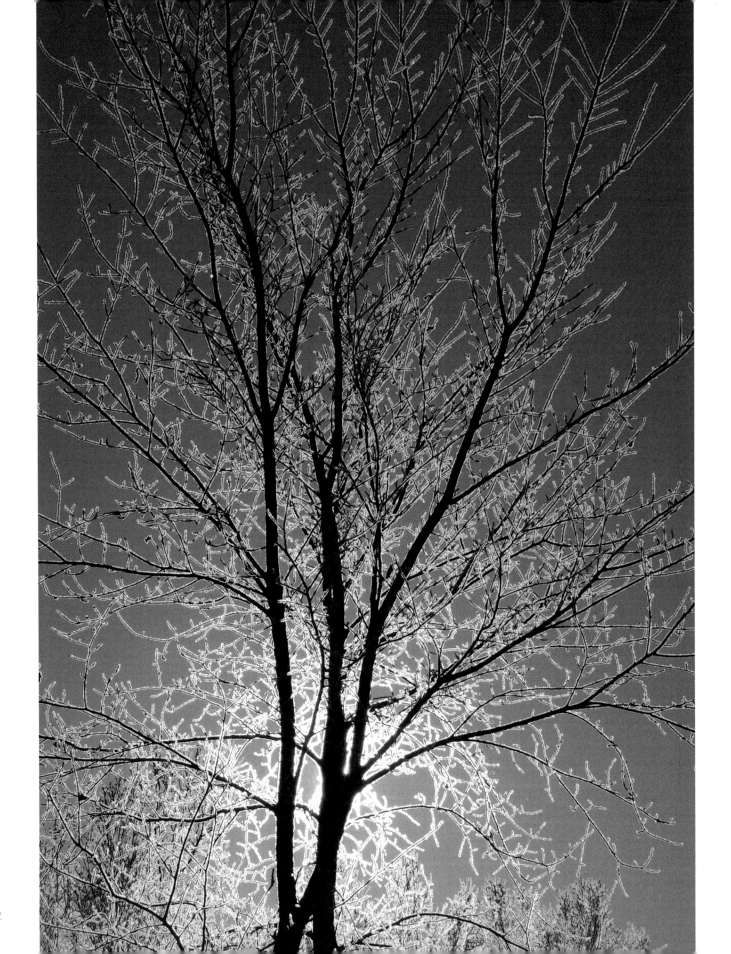

It is cold, clear, and still. My breath seems to hang in the air, and the absence of even a faint breeze makes the long walk down my driveway and back up again easy exercise. As I near my house, the sun's backlighting etches the frosted lines of a maple tree against the morning sky.

Over the years I've observed that no matter how cold the weather may be, when hoar frost rims the trees like this the temperature is going to climb above the freezing point within twenty-four to seventy-two hours. The frost often presages a storm as well. A related omen is the heavy sparking of hot coals when I shove new logs into my wood stove. When that happens, I know there's a storm coming for sure, regardless of what the weather office may be predicting.

Reading signs like these is uncommon these days. We're either too divorced from the natural world or too busy with everything else to pay attention. Certainly the little I've been able to observe makes me aware of how much I must be missing. And because everything in our biosphere is connected with and dependent on everything else, this lack of awareness bothers me. I want to participate more knowledgably in my environment, to know when and how to act, and when not to, for the good of us all. I'd like to be a more informed caretaker and a better gardener.

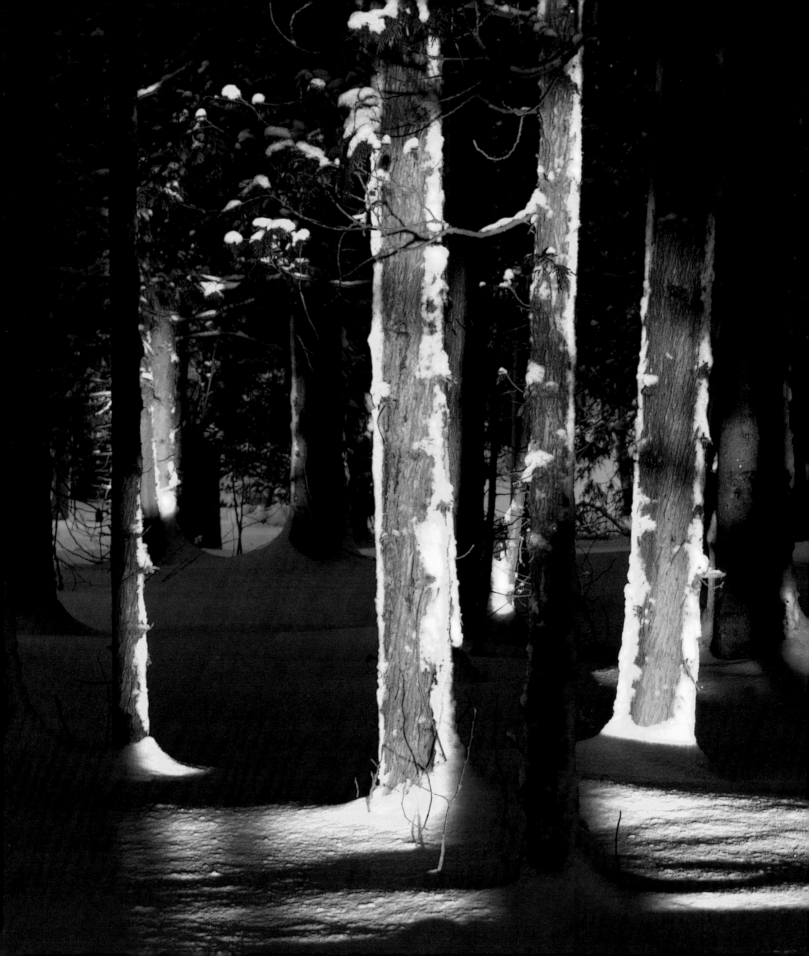

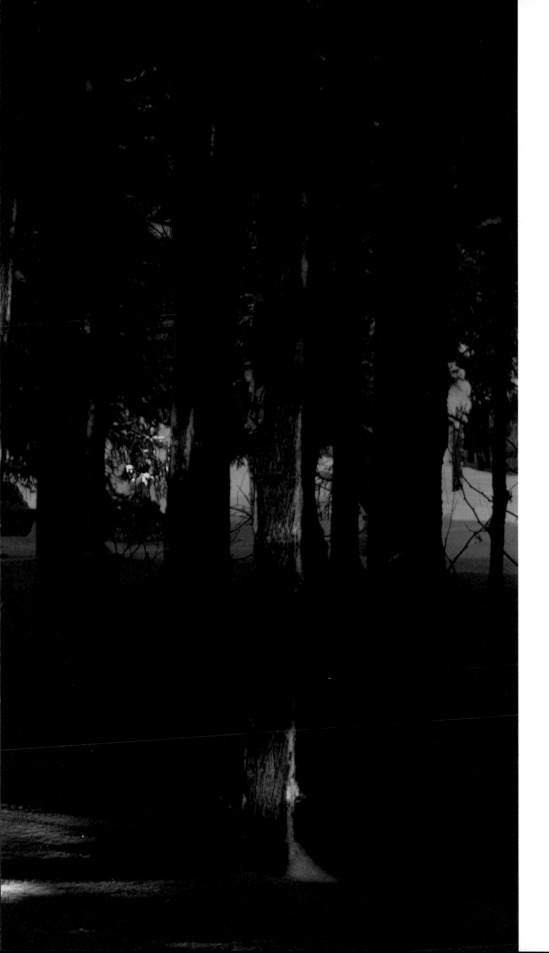

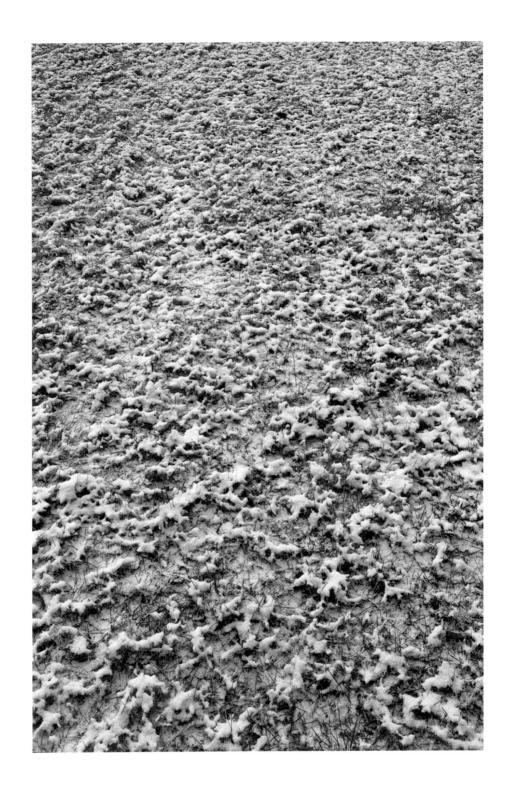

One cloudy-bright December morning

the tall grasses in the field behind my house, which had been battered down by a heavy snowfall, suddenly became visible again. The previous day's rain had melted the snow cover, but just before the storm ended the temperature had dropped enough to scatter a little fresh snow over everything, transforming the field into a tightly woven pattern of white flakes, mid-brown grasses, and tiny black shadows. Sheer texture — a tapestry!

I spent forty-five minutes on my deck with my lens aimed at small sections of the field, always avoiding any line or shape that was visually strong enough to draw attention to itself and away from the weave. The longer I photographed the more my sense of well-being grew. What was going on inside of me?

I suddenly realized that the texture was symbolic for me — a metaphor of my life at this point. All the good and bad experiences I'd had both at home and around the world, all the friendships I'd made and the difficult relationships I'd worked through were a weave, a fabric, a life, my life. I had been pointing my camera at a snowy field, but I was photographing myself.

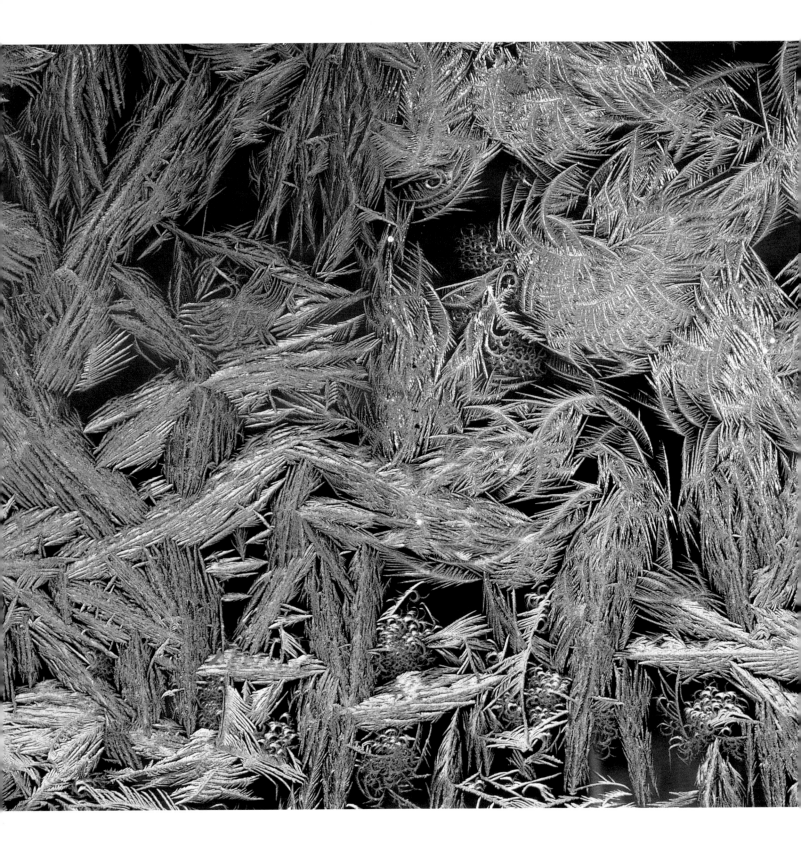

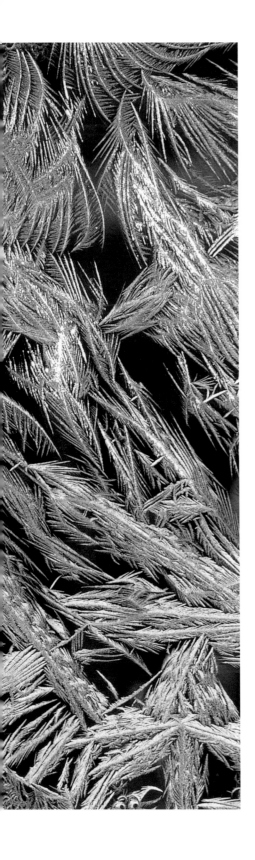

Goethe once described times in his life when he had fallen asleep in tears, but in his dreams the most charming forms had come to console and cheer him, and he had arisen the next morning fresh and joyful.

This frosty windowpane wasn't a dream, but its similarity to a very fine painting or tapestry is obvious, and its charming form transformed this morning. And, because the temperature remained below freezing, I was able to view it all day long.

The two single-pane windows in my house more than pay for the small heat loss by functioning as winter art exhibits. The display changes nearly every night.

Natural patterns are not art, just as a wild place is not a garden. Both art and gardens are created by human beings, and often express deeply felt human emotions, which natural patterns do not. There is, however, no other good reason to consider natural patterns as different in kind from human creations. Humans are part of nature too.

At Shamper's Bluff

I always look at ice with two possibilities in mind. Is the frozen area large enough and smooth enough for skating? And, are the bubbles and cracks of the ice patterns visually interesting? In other words, will I want to make photographs of them? The one possibility is as important to me as the other.

I photographed the patterns you see here on the flooded surface of a marsh. The ice area was certainly large enough for skating, but the surface was far too rough. So out came my camera instead — in late afternoon when winter sunlight was skimming across the ice, highlighting edges, and warming the color of marsh grasses.

Small ponds offer the same kind of visual opportunities, though every pond will be unique in its specific patterns — due to its microclimate and what is growing in and around it. So to have seen one pond is definitely not to have seen every one nearby. Because a pond in winter offers the observant eye a continually changing sequence of patterns, except when it is buried under snow, I feel that a gardener should include this reason among those that pertain to spring, summer, and fall when deciding whether or not to build a pond. After all, gardeners, like photographers, are visually oriented people, and our eyes do not suddenly fail us when the temperature drops below zero.

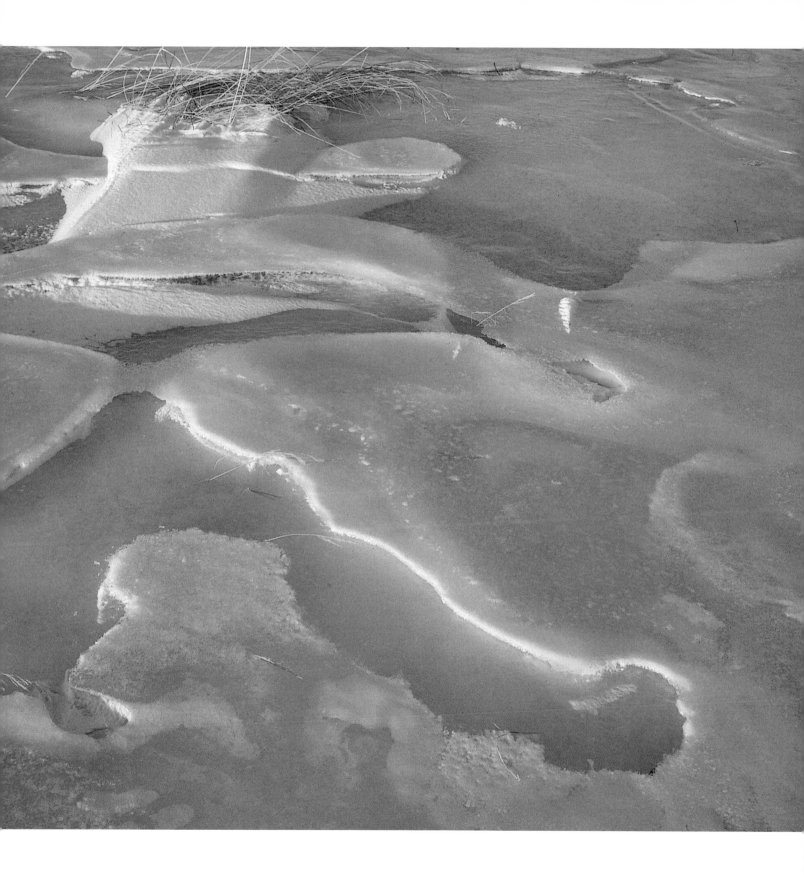

I photographed these patterns on the frozen surface of the St. John River, not far from the marsh shown on the preceding page or from my house on the hill. With an ice surface as smooth at this, you can be sure I was on skates. Very few people get the opportunity to enjoy naturally made ice, especially to skim long distances over the surface like a bird in flight. When I go round and round on an ice rink that is closed off from the sun, the moon, and the stars, heavenly objects that sometimes seem mirrored by the patterns of river or lake ice, I feel as if the bird has been caged.

The St. John River is influenced by the huge tides of the Bay of Fundy, and where I live, about twenty-five miles (forty kilometers) upriver from the ocean, the vast sheet of ice may rise or fall about a foot (a quarter or a third of a meter) every six hours. In the darkness of a moonless winter night, the lifting or dropping of the ice may crack the night air like a sharp thunderclap that reverberates far up the valley. The next day I may discover a long crack in the ice, visual evidence of that ominous, shattering sound.

Other cracks and holes appear in the ice surface, the causes of which I can only guess. Often, however, I am content for these formations to remain a mystery. To me they are intriguing as things-in-themselves, and I don't need to know how or why they came to be.

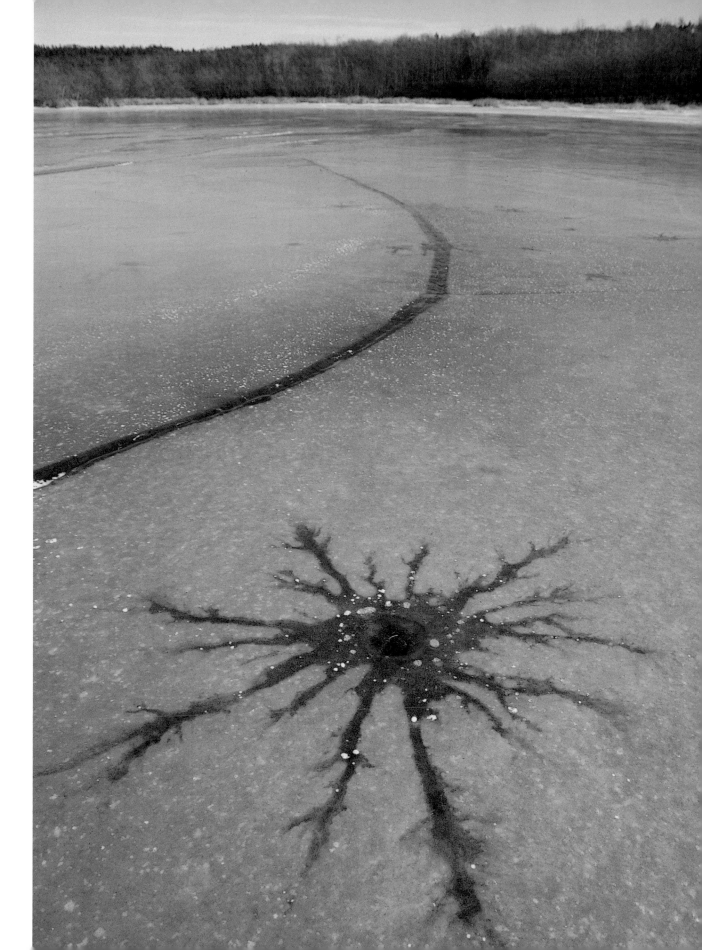

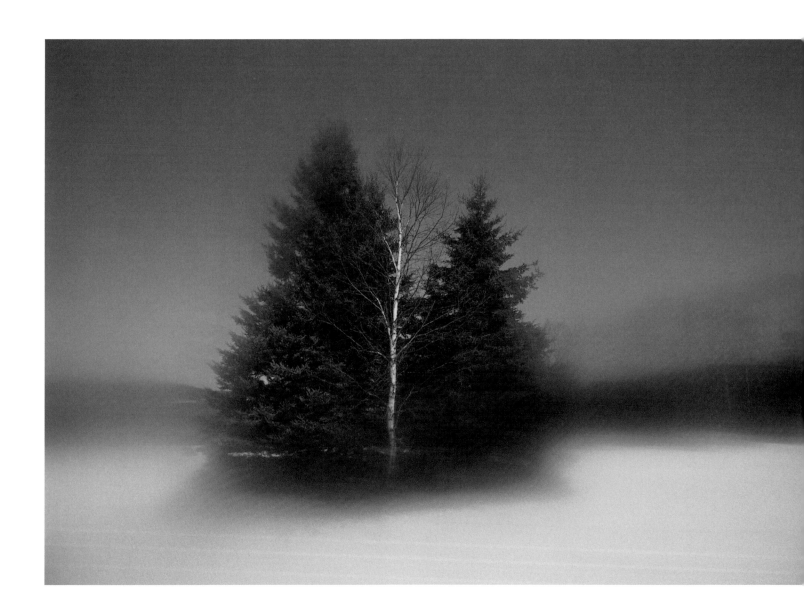

Walking down my long driveway one afternoon in March, I felt a compulsion to peer inside the tightly closed circle of seven spruce trees that stand tall and green in an open field. Was I sensing an invitation? Perhaps the frigid wind made me feel the trees would provide a warm shelter.

I waded through the remains of a snow bank, then pulled several heavy branches aside to enter the circle. There was a different world inside — a dead one. Intertwined gray branches reached from the frozen earth to a height of ten feet (three meters), their fallen brown needles strewn through remnant grasses. They had died from lack of light.

Forcing my way back through the outer branches, I struggled back to the road and headed up the hill to my barn. From a hook I chose an old handsaw, returned to the circle, and forced my way inside again. After two hours I had sawed away all the dead branches I could reach. The following afternoon I dragged them away and burned them. When I reentered the circle, I found a sanctuary, a place of peace. It's also like that when we look inside ourselves and decide to clear away all the dead wood.

I've placed two chairs inside my chapel. Usually I go there by myself and listen to birds singing. Invariably, I suck in the sweet fragrances of ferns and grasses, but mostly I just feel. Occasionally, I take along a bottle of fine wine and invite a friend to sit and share communion.

Flowering cabbage

and kale, whose appeal is in the appearance of their leaves, not that of their flowers, are among those plants whose beauty lingers late into autumn and often well into winter. The farther north you live, the more you should consider using them for ornamental plantings. Bothered less by snow, which insulates them, than by extreme cold, the plants form large, often immense, symmetrical rosettes of purple, pink, or white that blend to olive or grayish green near the base or stalk of the plant. Beautiful when unadorned, the leaves can only be described as "stunning" when their edges are studded with raindrops or rimmed with frost. When you interplant frilly-leaved varieties with the more usual types (one of which you see here), you can create an eye-stopper garden bed or a very dramatic border.

I enjoy flowering cabbage and kale most when they are covered with frost or peering through snow. They seem so defiant, yet very nonchalant. As I observe the pinkish rosettes emerging through a sea of white, I always get the feeling, "This can't be!" The scene defies my expectations, and thus challenges my ideas about the length of the gardening season, but having my assumptions challenged is invariably a good thing. Like most people, I often resent having nature inform me that things can be different from what I think or would like to assume. But, when I see these plants living in the snow, I never find the challenge hard to take.

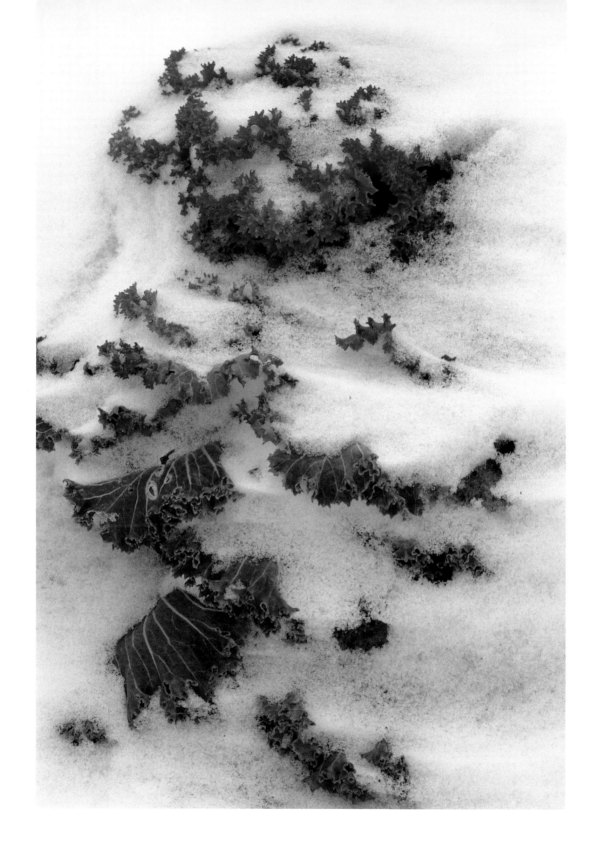

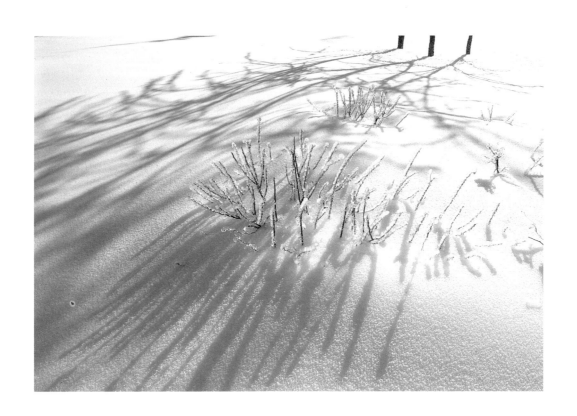

At the time I built my house I asked each of three
friends to plant a maple tree. The trees have grown well, and
now their interwoven branches form something of an orb,
green in the spring and summer, yellow orange in the fall, just
as I had hoped. However, I didn't even consider the possible
winter appearance of the trees, nor did I think about the
shadows their branches would cast across the snow on sunny
days. I didn't think about shadows when I planted the rose
bushes, either.

The composition of shadow lines is forever moving and
changing as the Earth rotates — slowly enough for me to
decide just when I most want to make some pictures. Because
of lighting conditions those times will vary. Some days and
at certain hours of the day, the warm or cool color of the
sunlight is as important as the lines themselves. Other times
I'm the changing factor, deciding to approach the shadows
from this direction or that, or perhaps tilting my camera
slightly to emphasize the orientation of the lines. I tend to
favor the oblique orientation that you see here, because
slanting lines always produce a sense of the dynamic —
suggesting movement, flow, and change.

Just about everybody complains about winter and
weather, especially about winter weather, and I'm no different.
But, perhaps we should all send up a little cheer when we see
shadows streaming so beautifully across the snow, and be
thankful for little unexpected gifts.

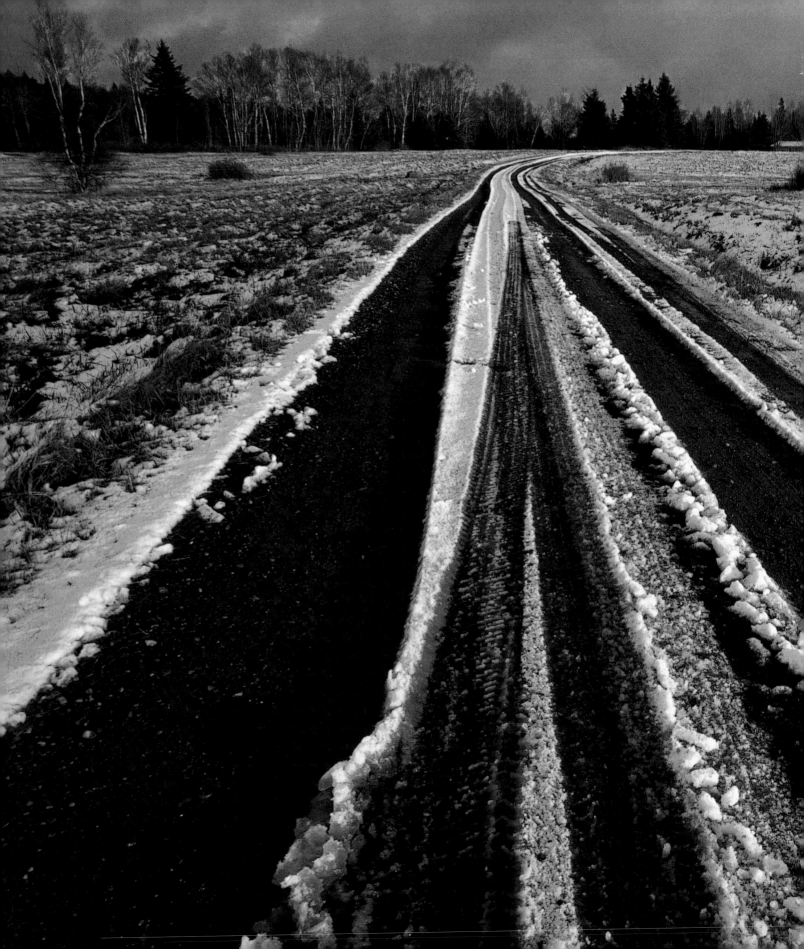

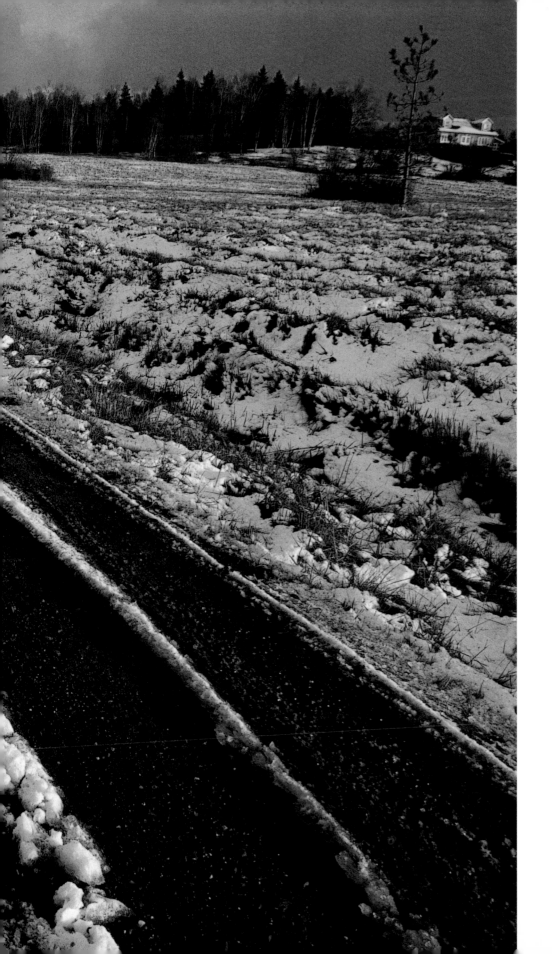

Most people who look at a photograph like this experience a sense of coziness and comfort induced by the warm hues of the lights shining in the blue winter twilight. While I can sense it too, there's a downside for me. I suffer from seasonal affective disorder, or SAD. Short hours of daylight and snow induce hibernation. When the main difference from one day to the next is the depth of snow in the fields and around the spruce and birch trees, I just want to go to bed. Other people can snowshoe and ski all they want, but most of the time I want no part of it.

The exceptions to my blues are those days, however cold, when I can find bare ground, perhaps after a rain or a high wind that piles up huge drifts by clearing snow from other parts of fields. When the ground is free of its white protective cover, so essential to the continuation of both plant and animal life, I feel liberated, because I can find mosses, lichens, and the remnants of last summer's leaves. It's a paradox, I realize, but that's just how it is, and no amount of light therapy or good intentions makes me feel otherwise. When half the world seems to have gone missing, I go into an emotional tailspin, or would if I couldn't keep on gardening.

This is why I have a sunroom-greenhouse, filled with ferns, clivia, orchids, jade plants, and zygocacti on the south end of my house. For me, gardening is a year-round activity.

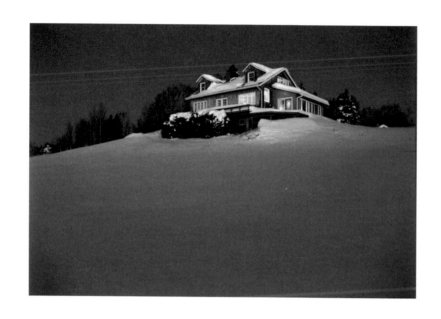

SPRING

We shall not cease from exploration

And the end of all our exploring

Will be to arrive where we started

And know the place for the first time

T.S. ELIOT, "Little Gidding"

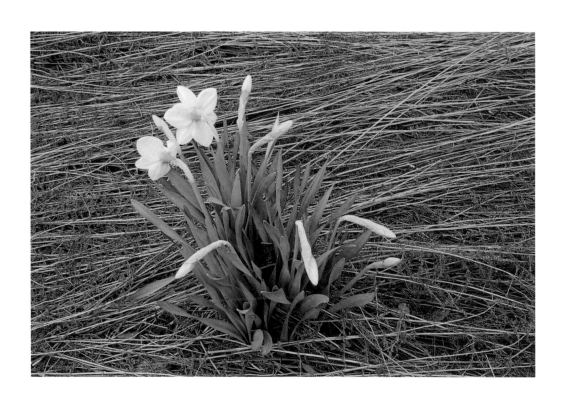

Eternity travels in circles. The seasons roll

around and around, and every year when the winds blow
warmer and mists swirl through the forests and over the
fields, the expectant Earth stirs, and with her life energy
begins the birthing process.

Catkins appear on aspens and birches. Sprightly, green
fern crosiers shove upward through the mulch of last year's
darkened fronds. In the meadow a new and vibrant generation
of daffodils, jonquils, narcissus — call them what you will —
begins to sway and dance, intent on celebration. And, once
again, the grass grows by itself.

I live out of doors in these days of arousal and
quickening, these days when everything good seems possible
again. I also live inside myself more powerfully than I have in
months, because I feel Earth's life energy kindling, creating,
birthing in me. I am inspired to journey out of doors and to
travel inward simultaneously, because spring is everywhere.

How can a person not garden in spring?

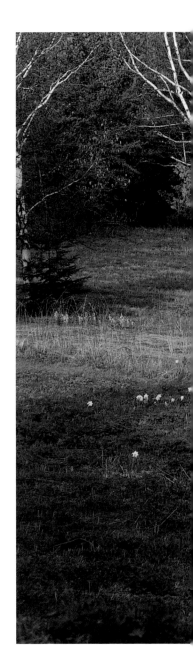

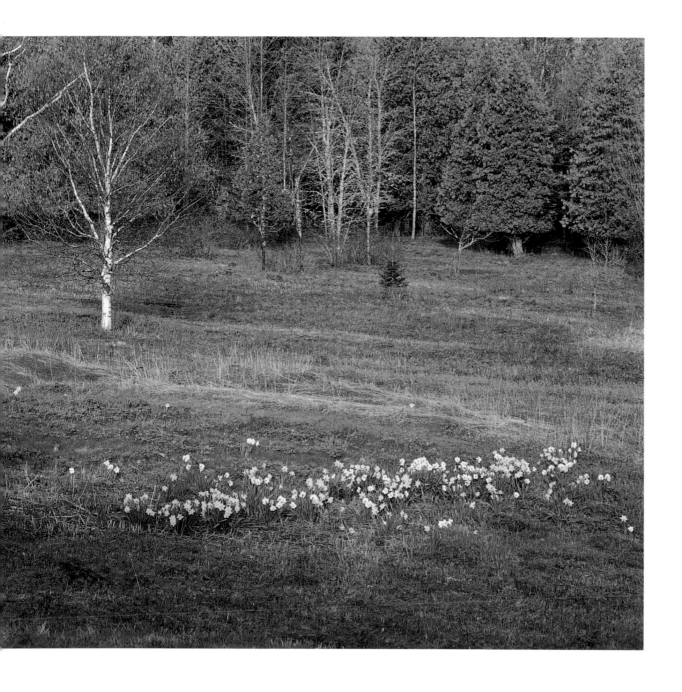

This is the end of your visit to my garden, and a good time to return to your own. The year has come full circle, and we and our gardens have circled with it. To rephrase Thomas Moore, our gardens and our souls cycle and twist, repeat and reprise. All of nature is echoing ancient themes.

Like every year, we have work to do — outside and inside. We have debris to collect and cart away to the compost heap, where it will mildew and rot and, with some spadework to turn it now and then, eventually become valuable humus for enriching the garden soil. We have perennials to divide and transplant, and extra clumps to set aside for friends and neighbors. We have shrubs to prune, hedges to clip, beds to dig, stones to remove, fertilizer to spread, and seeds to plant. And, as always, we will have weeds to pull. So let's go now and set to work, but not forget to "take time to smell the roses."

As you take your leave, think of me along a woodland path that leads through wild rhododendron bushes whose buds are just now coming to the moment of bloom. I will sit on the bench where I made this photograph, and listen again for the barely perceptible sound that seems to emanate from Heaven itself — the sound of a breeze moving through new leaves in the uppermost level of the forest canopy, my favorite aural expression of the coming of spring. And when I hear this music, I will believe again that everything good is possible.

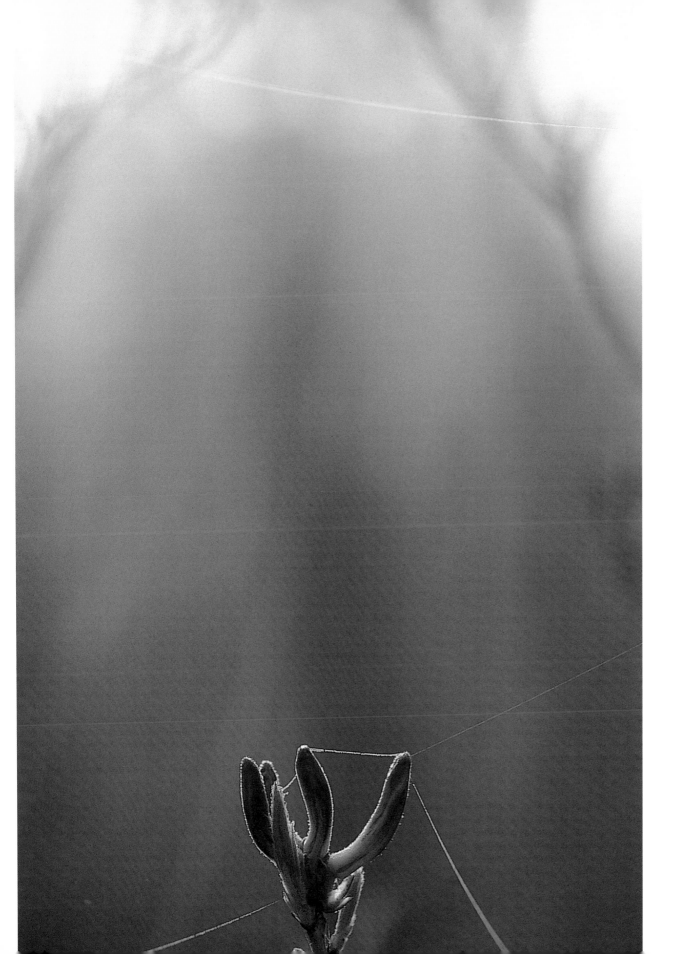

BOOKS BY FREEMAN PATTERSON

Photography for the Joy of It

Photography and the Art of Seeing

Photography of Natural Things

Photographing the World Around You

Namaqualand: Garden of the Gods

Portraits of Earth

The Last Wilderness: Images of the Canadian Wild

ShadowLight: A Photographer's Life

Odysseys: Meditations and Thoughts for a Life's Journey

Books with photography by Freeman Patterson

In a Canadian Garden by Nicole Eaton and Hilary Weston

Books by Freeman Patterson and André Gallant

Photo Impressionism and the Subjective Image

For more information on Freeman Patterson, his books, and his workshops in photography and visual design, please visit his web site at www.freemanpatterson.com.

BIOGRAPHY

FREEMAN PATTERSON lives at Shamper's Bluff, New Brunswick, near his childhood home. He has a bachelor's degree in philosophy from Acadia University and a master's degree in divinity from Union Seminary (Columbia University). He studied photography and visual design privately with Dr. Helen Manzer in New York. He began to work in photography in 1965, and numerous assignments for the Still Photography Division of the National Film Board of Canada followed.

In 1973 Freeman established a workshop of photography and visual design in New Brunswick, and in 1984 he co-founded the Namaqualand Photographic Workshops in southern Africa. He has given numerous workshops in the United States, Israel, England, New Zealand, and Australia. He has published eleven books and written for various magazines in Canada and the United States and for CBC radio. He has been featured on CBC television's *Man Alive*, *Sunday Arts and Entertainment*, and *Adrienne Clarkson Presents*. He was appointed to the Order of Canada in 1985.

Freeman was awarded the Gold Medal for Photographic Excellence from the National Film Board of Canada in 1967, the Hon EFIAP (the highest award) of the Fédération Internationale de l'Art Photographique (Berne, Switzerland) in 1975, honorary doctorates from the University of New Brunswick and Acadia University, the gold medal for distinguished contribution to photography from Canada's National Association for Photographic Art in 1984, and the Photographic Society of America's Progress Medal (the society's highest award; previous recipients include Ansel Adams, Eliot Porter, Jacques Cousteau, and the Eastman Kodak Company) in 1990.

In 2001 he received the Lifetime Achievement Award from the North American Nature Photography Association, and in 2003 he was awarded the Miller Britten Award for Excellence in the Visual Arts.